The Language Barrier

A handbook
for parents
and teachers

Order this book online at www.trafford.com/07-0678
or email orders@trafford.com

Most Trafford titles are also available at major online book retailers.

© Copyright 2007 Helen King.

All rights reserved. No part of this publication may be reproduced, stored in a retrieval system, or transmitted, in any form or by any means, electronic, mechanical, photocopying, recording, or otherwise, without the written prior permission of the author.

Note for Librarians: A cataloguing record for this book is available from Library and Archives Canada at www.collectionscanada.ca/amicus/index-e.html

Printed in Victoria, BC, Canada.

ISBN: 978-1-4251-2277-5

We at Trafford believe that it is the responsibility of us all, as both individuals and corporations, to make choices that are environmentally and socially sound. You, in turn, are supporting this responsible conduct each time you purchase a Trafford book, or make use of our publishing services. To find out how you are helping, please visit www.trafford.com/responsiblepublishing.html

Our mission is to efficiently provide the world's finest, most comprehensive book publishing service, enabling every author to experience success. To find out how to publish your book, your way, and have it available worldwide, visit us online at www.trafford.com/10510

www.trafford.com

North America & international
toll-free: 1 888 232 4444 (USA & Canada)
phone: 250 383 6864 ♦ fax: 250 383 6804
email: info@trafford.com

The United Kingdom & Europe
phone: +44 (0)1865 722 113 ♦ local rate: 0845 230 9601
facsimile: +44 (0)1865 722 868 ♦ email: info.uk@trafford.com

10 9 8 7 6 5 4 3

For Sarah, who talked me into writing this.

> Mrs Frayne
>
> All Erin's Year 6 teachers left today. Thankyou for all you have done for Erin, I will always be immensely grateful.
>
> Sarah.

Helen Khan
21.6.41 — 24.7.12

Contents

1.	Introduction	1
2.	How Language Can Be Seen as Power	5
3.	How Very Young Children Learn	7
4.	The 'Zone of Proximal Development'	11
5.	Motherese	14
6.	Early Speech	19
7.	Stages of Language Development In an Infant	22
8.	A Key Stage In Physical Development of Speech – The Dropped Epiglottis	25
9.	The Earliest Speech Sounds	30
10.	An Analysis of the First Fifty Words	34
11.	Towards Clearer Understanding	43
12.	The Naming Explosion	49
13.	Why It Is Difficult To Program a Computer to Speak Realistically	55
14.	Telegraphic Speech	58
15.	What Is It Like Being Speechless?	63
16.	So What Is Language?	67
17.	Baby Talk and Ancient Sumerian	72
18.	Some of the Elements of Language	78
19.	Very Young Children Question Language	81
20.	Physical Development and Language Development Are Related	85
21.	The Role of 'Emotional Response' In Speech	91
22.	Theories of Language: Skinner	97
23.	Children Have a Language Acquisition Device: Chomsky	100
24.	How Does It Feel To Be a Speechless Child?	103
25.	Bruner's LASS	106

26.	More Skilled Speakers Help Less Skilled.	110
27.	Growing Demands on The Child's Language.	114
28.	Learning to Read	117
29.	The Sense of Sight In a Child	121
30.	Games to Help Early Reading.	125
31.	An Analysis of Early Reading Steps	129
32.	Moving On to Writing.	133
33.	Children Acquire Culture Through Language	136
34.	How Language Influences the Way We See The World.	141
35.	The Benefits of Bilingualism	146
36.	Stephen Krashen.	150
37.	Between Two Languages	154
38.	Methods of Measuring Language Ability.	158
39.	BICS and CALP.	162
40.	BICS and CALP In a Monolingual Classroom	166
41.	A Lesson Where Children Use Language.	171
42.	Cracking The CALP Code	175
43.	Conclusion.	180

Chapter One
_____

Introduction

Most children understand and speak language by the time they start school, usually at age five.

Research has been done which shows that even in early infancy, babies show a preference for language over other sounds. At a few weeks old they also show a preference for the sounds of their mother tongue from the sounds of a foreign one, and after a few weeks, they can distinguish sounds of their native language from other tongues.

Most babies speak their first words from some time roughly between their first birthday and eighteen months of age. The same child by the age of four, can be learning an average of ten words a day!

Learning words in isolation however is not learning a language. There are set ways to place these words in a sentence to carry a specific meaning. Say, you take a sentence like, 'The cat chased the dog.'

Using the exact same words in a different order alters the original meaning completely. The dog chased the cat.

So children learn not only words but the rules needed to order them – which is grammar– to give an intended meaning.

> *How do children understand these rules?*
> *How do they understand the meaning of words?*
> *How does a child learn mother tongue?*

There are many great names in the field of language and linguistics. People like Chomsky, Krashen, Sapir, Whorf, Cummins, Halliday,

The Language Barrier

Skinner, Vygotsky, Wells, Bruner and many others have contributed hugely to our knowledge of language development in children. They offer exciting insights, and fresh light on teaching and learning. I have used their research and perceptions to prompt my own thinking and observations.

If you want to read their work in the original, just type their name and the word 'language ' into a search engine on the nearest computer you can find! I still find it hard to believe that I have this incredible tool available to me at the touch of a few buttons on a keyboard.

In a book of this kind I think you should know a little about the writer. I have five children, now grown up with independent lives of their own. When I was younger I taught in secondary schools, mainly in the London area. In my later years of teaching I became increasingly involved in designing lessons to help bilingual pupils. This forced me to look more closely at the role of language in learning. These lessons compel a teacher to look very hard at *exactly* what they are teaching, whatever the subject.

Not only must they ensure that the pupil grasps the idea of the lesson itself, but also that the learner must be given the language skills necessary to express this understanding.

I am retired from teaching, but as yet not from learning, or should I say acquiring, knowledge!

One of my daughters manages her own business, so when she had her own daughter, Erin, I took over the majority of childminding during the working week.

I decided that the inevitable monotony and tedium of regular infant minding would be livened up a little if I did a study of this new grandchild's language development.

Erin and I have had a very full and enjoyable few years together, and watching her, and how her language skills grew, led to more understanding of language. The trouble is that when you are teaching you have little time for reflection. Grandmothers have much more thinking time!

As a teacher I was fortunate to discover early on in my career that a period of quiet reflection after a lesson, whether successful or not, was time well spent. What is successful? The learners are engaged in learning, happy, and acquiring new skills or knowledge or both.

If successful, why? And can I replicate this in the future?

If a failure, why? What can I do to improve this in future?

Introduction

After all teachers are pragmatists. And if a class are happily engaged in work there are no behavioural problems to deal with. So life in school is happier for both teacher and pupil.

Equally, if a child at home is happy most of your problems are solved. I would do a lot to avoid a whiney, grizzly infant.

I made notes on much of Erin's early language acquisition. I use them in this text as not everyone reading this may have had first hand experience of bringing up a child, and even if you have had you may not remember too well the sequence of events. I have tried to include general comment on learning and language to set the child's words in context. It seems to me that as she is an actual child, (i.e. not a theoretical 'norm'!) and the acquisition sequence is as recorded, then she might help to illustrate some of the theory we will explore later. We need some facts before we can explore and evaluate theory.

I know that there have been very valuable studies done by others in recording and analysing children's speech in an attempt to understand the threads in the story of how it all happens. In the course of my own observations I have had immense fun, and made many discoveries which have enhanced my view of humans as absolutely amazing creatures right from the earliest days of childhood.

I have also gained a much deeper understanding of the abilities of infants. That word is interesting in itself – infant. It comes from a root word meaning 'before speech' or 'speechless'!

From what I have seen and I'm sure most other people engaged with infants can see for themselves, the infant may be speechless but they can certainly communicate! We tend not to notice gesture, grunts, gurgles, laughs, cries and so on as language, but of course they are important communication tools.

And as far as it goes when I quote research it is always the research which I have observed to actually 'work' in real life. The research is accurate as far as I have experienced using it. I do not want to take credit from the earlier researchers in linguistics, but I do want people – especially parents, child minders and teachers – to understand the incredibly significant role played by written and spoken language in the creation of our personal worlds. By personal world I mean our understanding of, our participation in, all kinds of relationships, with family, friends, people we meet, television we watch, radios stations we listen to, papers we read and so on. Whatever builds up our individual universe.

Let me make this point of view clearer. Much new research keeps appearing in the public eye about how children learn. Sometimes it seems to me that people go overboard with one theory or another and forget to use their common sense. Such as a friend of my daughter ringing to tell her that she had read that playing classical music to babies made baby into a genius.

Therefore that Erin should have Mozart, Bach and Beethoven constantly playing in the background. The reasoning was along the lines of listen to the works of genius and release your child's undiscovered genius. Anyway as it happened Erin did listen to classical music.

Occasionally.

When I fancied a change from nursery rhymes.

Still when I heard the enthusiasm for Mozart I thought about it. It seemed to echo the research done into the effect of classical baroque music on the human brain. Such music slows the heartbeat to time with the music, and relaxes the listener so that the mind is clear, and capable of facing learning with renewed vigour.

I took a look at Erin's then current musical input. She was aged 2.1

She loved Pavorotti's arias and threw herself heart and soul into bellowing 'ba ba ba ba', accompanied by very extravagant hand gestures and facial expressions. I found this very amusing as she had never watched opera, but seemed to have an empathy with the sound, and realised that here was passion and high drama!

Equally she loved to dance to pop music, imitating the latest dance crazes she saw on music channels of television. Once in central Manchester she was so transfixed by a huge band, all of whom were beating out insistent rhythms on drums, that I bought the cd they were selling so she could continue to enjoy such music at home. A far cry from Mozart's disciplined beat and counter beat.

And she was in seventh heaven dancing the 'hokey cokey' or the conga with her parents and grandparents. I could see that dancing to pop music she was learning rhythm and balance, as well as engaging in enjoyable social activities with others.

So we continued with her mixed musical diet.

So if you differ with me on things I write, or want to know more about where I'm coming from, then use any search engine on the internet.

For example on this issue of music and genius type in key words. Maybe 'music' 'child' 'genius'. Then see what you get!

I've actually just done this myself and been intrigued and amused to find that genius can be, and often is, labelled as 'abnormality'.

Chapter Two

How Language Can Be Seen As Power

What we know so far about how a child acquires home language is well documented, and is still very much ongoing. You can see an account of this research a little further on in the text.

For now it is enough to agree that most children, with varying degrees of proficiency, can speak and understand mother tongue by age five without any formal teaching taking place.

Since the mid nineteenth century there has been an ever increasing volume of research and theory available on language, learning and thought. In my career as a teacher I needed to understand as well as I could the interconnections between language and intellectual development. In my own studies at the time one thing which struck me forcibly was the insistence on the use of abstruse language to convey meaning. It seemed to me that many academics thought that the more obscure the writing, the more of an expert the writer was thought to be in his or her particular field. It was often very frustrating to bore (in every sense!) through mountains of often abstract 'academic language' to find the final kernel of information you were looking for.

Bearing that in mind I have in writing this allowed clarity in expressing an idea quite often to invade on precision. However, aware of many 'loose' expressions I use I would point out that today the internet is there for everybody. As far as I am aware I name the source of all the ideas I write about here so that all you would have to do is use a search engine to get the original thesis or lecture to clarify anything you believe to be obscure.

You will find that more recent researchers, that is, from the 80s on, do seem to be getting more user friendly in addressing their readers.

In the 21st century a child needs to be fluent and competent in language.

From what I see, language, or the control and use of language, is power. Or perhaps more importantly, language is the tool whereby you will be safe and strong against the power of others who may not always desire your best good. This empowering exists at both a local and global level. Within a community individuals need the ability to use language to facilitate daily life, and to deal with inevitable daily upsets or setbacks.

At global level some of the world's languages are far more powerful than others. The U.N. for example, publishes in only six 'official' languages, whereas it purports to represent speakers of scores of other; what are referred to as 'minority' languages. As their organisation says, 'The Organization uses six official languages in its intergovernmental meetings and documents, Arabic, Chinese, English, French, Russian and Spanish; the Secretariat uses two working languages, English and French.

Statements made in an official language at a formal meeting are interpreted simultaneously into the other official languages of the body concerned by United Nations interpreters. If a delegation wishes to speak in a language that is not an official language, it must supply an interpreter to interpret the statement or translate it into one of the official languages. It is then rendered into the other languages by a relay system.'

Even the use of terms like **'*official*'** and **'*minority*'** carry overtones of political power structures and the ranking of individual states within them.

In much the same way within a language those with the best verbal skills tend to outdo those who struggle to express their ideas and feelings. This fact of life is shown in phrases like 'dumb blonde', when 'dumb' is understood as the equivalent of stupid or empty headed.

Therefore parents and teachers should really work to empower every child with efficient and fluent language, both spoken and written.

I, probably like all teachers, have my own ideas of what works or not in teaching!

From my experience it seemed to me that the best learning takes place when the teacher *provides a situation* within which learning can take place. The teacher knows, or to be more accurate *should* know, at what stage of learning the child is; and be able to prepare a situation in which the child will progress further.

The teacher becomes more of a facilitator of learning, a consultant, ready to answer questions as and when they arise, within the learning situation which the teacher has devised. This does not in any way mean that they abdicate their role of wiser adult, of one ultimately in control of the learning environment.

But they are willing to empower the child.

Just like Mums and Dads do automatically all the time. Except that parents also, especially in play and talk, often *anticipate* need and fill the gap before the child is even aware that help is needed. I see it as a sign of really active learning when the pupil questions the teacher more than vice versa.

Children who are *involved* in play make the best progress.
Children who ask questions actually *want* to know the answers.

Research has been done which shows that more than 80% of success for children *in* school is due to factors *outside* school! These factors include the amount and quality of play and other experiences the preschool child has had, the child's natural intelligence, the amount of 'scaffolding' his home background has provided for learning of every kind, and so on.

Moreover equally interesting is the result of further research called the 'Matthew effect'. This demonstrates that the better equipped a child is for school the faster he will progress in school, the less well equipped the more he will fall behind. Mind you, if you pause and think about this, it *is* pretty obvious! But to my mind, that is to me one of the problems with academic conclusions. No one is allowed to state the obvious unless there is verifiable research evidence to support the view.

In this writing here, however, I write as I see the truth about these issues, whether I am aware of corroborative research or not. Where there is such research I point you in the direction of enough key words to find all you need to know on the internet.

Chapter Three

How Very Young Children Learn

When we play with children we very often *show* them what we want them to do. For example when a child first gets building bricks, we let them play with them for a while, letting the child feel the bricks, look at them, maybe even chew them a bit to get as much information as possible from these new objects in the toy box. We let them use all their senses to check out things for themselves. You all know the stage in development when it seems that everything goes straight in the child's mouth!

We must try not to forget as they grow older that all the senses can still contribute to learning, opening new and more pathways to the child's brain. A piece of information learned through more than one sense (in more than one sense!) is far more deeply understood by the learner.

This fact is at last getting some more formal recognition in the development of research into learning styles at all levels of education, from kindergarten to university, and even beyond.

Soon with the new bricks we maybe put one on top of another. We know that you can build with bricks and we demonstrate the fact. We show that you can place one brick on top of another. Maybe the child knocks them down. And initially there is more building up by an adult or an older child, and more knocking down by the learner.

Gradually however, the toddler tries one brick on another, often failing to balance them but quite engrossed in the task. A helpful adult will maybe hold the bottom brick steady to enable the toddler to succeed. Eventually the child will succeed in balancing the two bricks. The adult will most likely then build with three bricks, to encourage the child to build higher. And so on.

Eventually the adult will have demonstrated quite complex structures of bricks, maybe one bridging two lower ones and so on. Of course the child's progress with the bricks will be spread over many weeks, even months.

Even when the skill of building is mastered the child may return now and then to play with them and experience again the pleasure of building them up and knocking them down. And at any time the child gets bored with the bricks and abandons them for some other activity, we accept this and put them away for another day.

As in all learning activities the basics are repeated several times before anything more complicated is attempted. As adults we still have much of this childhood fascination with building bigger structures out of smaller ones. We start with a slight interest in a topic – and gradually build up an in depth knowledge of those subjects which interest us.

The way a child plays with bricks gives some important pieces of information about learning.

Even though the child is not yet using the same kind of language as the adult, and no one expects him to, the adult is usually constantly describing what is happening.

'You like your new bricks do you? Mummy bought you some nice bricks. Can we build with these bricks? Let's see. Oh that's good. Oh! They've fallen down. Let's try again. We put this one on this one. Did you knock them down? Oh! Do you want to try yourself? Very good. Oh! it fell off. Let's try again. '

You know the kind of talk yourself.

But now notice the very clever teaching strategies at work:-

The adult constantly describes what is happening *here and now*. The child's passive or silent vocabulary is growing as we speak the words to describe the activity. You will know that the child is learning the word 'bricks' when you say some day, 'Do you want to play with your bricks?' and the child – who as yet has never used the word 'brick himself – looks round for them, and fetches them, from amongst a collection of other toys. He understands the word 'bricks'. He may not yet have spoken the word but he certainly understands it.

While apparently 'playing' you are teaching your child to speak. You are also teaching about solid shapes, and balancing, and building. He is learning to hold, place things, how to coordinate hand and eye movements.

You may mention the colour of the brick, or talk about the pictures on the sides. All new information for the child.

As soon as the child masters one step the adult introduces one at a slightly more advanced level of difficulty. We ***show and say*** what can be done. First two bricks, then three. This is target setting carefully based on what you know of the child's level of ability.

You are providing the essential 'scaffolding' a child needs to learn. Jerome Bruner, an eminent cognitive psychologist, describes it in this way:

Scaffolding is the process of transferring skill, whereby an adult supports a child in learning a new task and gradually withdraws control as the child gains mastery.

You do not formally teach.
You provide the perfect conditions for learning to 'happen'.
You offer achievable targets.
You do not worry whether the target is achieved today or not.

You are relaxed, and enjoying your child's pleasure in play (alias learning!) The child is learning more and more refined skills, how to hold things, how to balance them. How to persevere until mastery of a task is achieved.

The child sets the pace of the activity. The adult responds to the child's interest. After all on a purely practical level, the more we facilitate the child's ability to cope for himself and make him independent of us, the quicker we will have some free time to get on with our own interests!

Chapter Four

The 'Zone of Proximal Development'

The kind of learning taking place with the bricks example above was first analysed and explained by a Russian psychologist named Vygotsky. He said that the best learning occurs within what he termed the child's 'zone of proximal development'. This is known as the ZPD for short.

He defined this as—

'the distance between the actual developmental level as determined by independent problem solving and the level of potential development as determined through problem solving under adult guidance or in collaboration with more capable peers.'

That is to say, it is the difference between what a child can do unaided and what he can do if he is given appropriate assistance.

The importance of the ZPD for those teaching a child is that it defines the upper and lower boundaries within which the teaching should take place. Parents and carers seem to know this without much hesitation. They wouldn't for example give bricks to a three month old child to play with because they would understand that in order to play the child needs to be able to sit up independently, and to reach out, grasp and move a brick to where he wants it.

Neither would they expect a toddler to do a complicated jigsaw. There is always a challenge in play but it must be a challenge that the child can meet, initially with help, and later independently.

As Vygotsky puts it—

'Instruction is only useful when it moves ahead of development leading the child to carry out activities which force him to rise above himself.'

So initially the parents encourage the babbling of an infant by constantly cooing baba, mama and so on until the infant can successfully do this himself. The infant is being led into realising that control of his own babbling leads to pleasure in his minders and consequently praise and treats for himself. So he masters the task. Later this will become far more sophisticated such as when you have mini dialogues with a toddler. He may say, 'Teddy chair', and an adult responds, "Yes. Teddy is sitting on his chair."

Always ahead, but only slightly ahead of the child.

As Vygotsky points out—

'Instruction takes on forms that are specific to each age level.'

That is to say effective teaching and learning take place when instruction matches exactly the ability level of the learner.

Neither does Vygotsky ignore the role of the *setting* in which learning takes place. He wrote—

'Human leaning presupposes a specific social nature and a process by which children grow into the intellectual life of those around them.'

It is easy enough to see that learners need a guide and this presupposes a **social** setting. No child can learn to talk in a vacuum, in a world of no communication. It is pretty obvious that if there is not talk around him and to him, he cannot possibly suddenly burst into speech! Initially this social setting is the home, then perhaps nursery, friends, neighbours, relatives, then school.

At first, in life the social setting of learning is obvious, and very often one to one dialogue accompanies activities. Communication is through the spoken word alone, accompanied by body language gesture, intonation and facial expression.

Quite early on this changes – especially for the modern child. Television and computers are expected to be part of the communication process.

So as we grow older books, television programmes, DVDs, CD Roms, magazines, newspapers and so on can undertake the role of teacher. This may seem learning outside a social setting but of course someone, somewhere has written or produced the source from which we now learn. So there is always the human social element in learning.

Equally it is reasonable to see learning as an ongoing ***process*** in life. We never reach a stage when we can safely say, 'I have now learned everything I am ever going to know in life!'

To my mind it is the earliest teachers of a child, those who look after him from birth until he starts at school or nursery, who are the most able

The 'Zone of Proximal Development'

to implement Vygotsky's analysis of the perfect setting for optimum progress.

They know *exactly* at what stage of development the child is.

They know precisely his limits and possibilities. So using this knowledge they are highly successful in their teaching. Perhaps this is because both teacher and learner are almost unaware of the work that is going on here.

This reminds me of a conversation with Erin just turned five years of age. I had bought a kit to make a metal rose arch for the garden. I asked the child to help me to assemble it. We undid the packaging and set to sorting the metal components and screws, and beginning construction. Soon we had it all worked out where different bits went and how to assemble them.

The child said, 'You put the right bits together and I'll do the screws.'

As we worked on and one side of the arch grew before our eyes, she remarked, 'This is fun Grandma!' Then she paused, and asked, 'Is it fun or is it work?' I had to admit that I wasn't sure. It was certainly a job I wanted doing, but we were also really enjoying ourselves. It certainly didn't feel like work. I told the child what I thought, and added, 'Maybe if you're doing what you love doing it's fun, if you don't want to do it and have to do it maybe it's work. I don't really know.'

I felt that at 5.0 she was old enough to know that mistakes or wrong answers are O.K. and not the end of the world!

She was silent for a while. Maybe she was considering the problem still – work or play?

Maybe she was thinking, 'Goodness! Grandma doesn't know.'

Finally she said, 'Well I think the same! Maybe we are both right and maybe we are both wrong. But it *is* fun!'

I think a lot of early learning for a child is like this. They are working extremely hard right from birth but they are also enjoying themselves. No one says, 'Today I am going to *teach* you how to say 'Mama'! They just do it.

Anyway formal teaching is counterproductive with very young children. Parents are very successful teaching a child to talk because they do not formally teach in any way. However they work very hard at informal teaching, at creating the opportunities for learning to take place. They are creating a perfect Vygotsky Zone of Proximal Development for the child!

Chapter Five

Motherese

When the child is initially breaking through into speech others do not correct 'mistakes'.

Anyway research shows that this wouldn't work.

There is, for example, what linguists call the 'fis phenomenon'. It shows the difference between what a child *hears* and what he can *say*. A child was playing with a plastic fish, and calling it his 'fis'. The conversation went like this.

Adult. 'This is your fis?'

Child. 'No, my fis'.

The adult spoke a little more but each time he called the fish 'fis' the child corrected him. 'Fis.'

Finally the adult said, 'That is your fish.'

'Yes,' agreed the child, 'my fis.'

We see from this that children know what they are aiming for in speech. The fact that the child couldn't as yet achieve it did not mean that he was unaware of incorrect pronunciation. He understands how the word *should* be pronounced but as yet has insufficient command over the actual physical controls needed for production. In this example once the adult pronounced the word the way the child knew it should be pronounced the child was satisfied.

A famous sentence in a government report on education is,

'Begin where the child is'.

To begin a piece of learning at a stage perfectly matched to the individual child must be very hard for teachers in reception classes.

They cannot know a child as well as his parents know him. Parents or carers know a child, and know what understanding and skills he has at any moment. They can organise play which will develop these skills and understanding. They develop a child's speaking skills as they talk about what they are doing. They are providing the words which the child will come across later in situations outside the home.

Therefore, to my mind, a really good nursery will provide an in depth interview and questionnaire for parents.

If it doesn't how can the teachers know where to begin?

Later on a teacher will have a far better idea of progress as the child will have reports from previous classes or previous schools.

But at this first crucial encounter with the formal education system many children are plunged into nursery classrooms where no one has bothered to find out what he can or cannot do.

As with all healthy children for Erin learning to speak was not a chore, neither was it so for me. Her family members around her spoke and the child listened, and gradually as the linguists say language 'emerged'.

'Children learn language not by rote, but by a seemingly effortless interaction between their sponge-like brains and their language-rich environments.'[Christopher A. Turber]

The child's brain had been accessed through hearing sounds, and gradually making sense of them.

And in fact recent research in child development shows that hearing is very well developed in infants. However newborn infants still cannot hear as well as adults. They cannot hear any of those very soft and gentle sounds which would be audible to an adult.

Decibels are used to measure how loud a sound is, and research shows that sounds must be roughly 10 to 17 decibels louder for an infant to hear it than for an adult. Great if you are trying to get them asleep!

Sounds which are within the frequency range of the average human voice are the sounds which infants are most sensitive to. Parents seem to understand this almost intuitively as the tones of voice used speaking to a baby are normally higher than those used in normal everyday conversation. At about two years of age however most children have reached adult levels of hearing.

So it is in response to the child's level of development – his ZPD – that people have responded when they use what most people call 'baby' talk, but linguists refer to as 'motherese' or 'caretaker speech'.

This is very important in a child's language development – those short, higher pitched, repetitive things adults say to infants. And the remarkable thing is that these 'conversations' start as soon as the baby is born – long before there is any remote possibility of a *language* response from the child. Though there is quite a definite behaviour response.

Like in any adult talk the mother allows pauses for baby's reply to her communication and accepts all sorts of coos, gurgles, sounds and grunts, as well as body movements, as responses to what she is saying.

"Do you want a bottle then? Does baby want a bottle? Mummy's getting the bottle for baby! Here we are! Here's the baby's bottle."

Crying or wailing turns to gurgling as baby sees Mum set about getting food!

Another thing to notice here is that 'motherese' talks all the time about what is happening here and now. The talk concerns things of immediate interest to the child and refers to familiar everyday items in the lives of child and minding adult.

You very likely know yourself the kind of daily conversation which takes place in this way. Maybe not strictly a dialogue, in the sense that the child doesn't answer, and isn't expected to really, except in coos and babbles, or if he is very hungry and cross, cries!

However the parent isn't put off by this as experience has shown us that eventually such 'motherese' pays off. It is a wonderful time in parents' lives when they see that their child is starting to make sense of the spoken word.

This can come about in all sorts of ways.

For example, I knew that when I said things like, 'Do you want a bottle Erin?' or, 'Do you want to go out in your pram?' to my then 15 month old granddaughter she was not going to verbalise a reply to me. But if she moved to where her bottle was usually prepared in the kitchen, or hurried to her pushchair that was answer enough to my question. As the linguists would say, I was getting an action response to a verbal request!

Very exciting times.

She was starting to understand us!

I expected, and accepted like all adults, that a child will be 'silent' for a long time before they actually produce a spoken response though it is perfectly obvious that their brain has understood spoken language as a means of communication.

I put silent in inverted commas in that last sentence because the child will not be really silent, in the sense of not making a sound.

I mean that the earliest childish babble is unintelligible to the average listener!

Even when speech does emerge it is probably only understood by those close to the child who are responsible for her everyday world. And this is one of the greatest things about human language that often goes unnoticed by many.

Speech demands a listener, a sympathetic listener, willing to use all sorts of clues to interpret the meaning of sounds.

Again using Erin as an illustrator here, and using three different sounds she made each starting with the same – easy to learn for small children – letter 'b'. These sounds were 'bay', 'boh' and 'bah'. For immediate family this was easy to understand!

'bay' meant that she would like someone to put on a video showing one of her favourite characters at that time, a bear. 'Bear in the big blue house.'

'boh' was a request for a bottle, and 'bah' meant that she would quite like a splash in the bath!

Everyone was delighted with this daily emerging speech, and it never crossed anyone's mind that quite intensive teaching was going on. The 'bay' was listened to and a response made, which would include frequent repetitions of the key word. You know what I mean.

'Oh! you want to watch bear do you? Now where is bear? Let's see if we can put on the bear video. Bear should come on in a minute. Ah, here he is! Here's bear!' and so on.

What is significant here is that it was ***vowel change*** which altered meaning. And that Erin realised this herself, that is, she never confused the sound/sense when using them.

Bay
Bah
Boh

Erin was really coming to grips with language.

Similar situations occur daily in the life of any child learning to speak.

Another point which is probably worth noticing here is that not only mother's change their normal speech patterns to talk to baby, but that fathers do too. However 'fatherese' seems to be slightly different in that it tends to be more demanding of the infant, with more questions, and a wider range of vocabulary than the mother would tend to use.

Indeed this was true of Erin's dad, who at a very early age, excited by her developing communication skills, said things to her like, 'Erin, say, "I love daddy", but, since Erin seemed to accept this in her stride, all was well.

Of course she didn't say, 'I love daddy' at that stage. But by amazing persistence on both their parts she started getting somewhere. Her dad's teaching went like this.

> 'Erin, say, "I".'
> Erin responded, 'I'.
> 'Love'.
> She had a bash at it.
> 'Daddy'.
> 'Daddy'.

There was a bit of a hiccup because this game went on so long that soon, as soon as she said 'I', she followed with a triumphant, 'Daddy'.

It seemed to me that language learning as such was not going on here, but both Erin and her Dad, Damien, were enjoying a game, in which Erin was keen to please her dad. I didn't see how she could say 'I love dad', and mean it, since she didn't know the meaning of the word 'love' as yet. That is not to say she didn't love her dad, she most certainly did.

But her dad was trying 'formal' teaching at too young an age and it just couldn't work. However, she was learning valuable interpersonal skills. She loved her dad, and recognised that if she could possibly complete the – to her crazy – task he was setting her he would be pleased. So she did her best to please.

An amusing bit of sign language developed from this. When Damien realised that the verbal communication wasn't getting there, he substituted a sign version. He would say 'I' and point to his eye; then 'love' accompanied by his hands clasped over his heart; finally with 'you', he would point to Erin.

She grasped this very quickly, and every morning as he left for work she would go to the window and 'sign' her message to him.

Though she has long since learned the words they both use the same signs to the present day.

Chapter Six

Early Speech

All parents know that a child's 'silent', or 'unspoken' vocabulary will be far greater than the 'surface', or 'productive' vocabulary, that is the words which the child at any stage is actually using in speech. Mothers of babies and toddlers are usually delighted when they note how much the child *understands* of daily life without the child saying much, if indeed anything at all, or at least anything comprehensible! The child can *demonstrate* understanding because of developing motor ability.

Research with bilinguals shows that it takes an average of five months for a child, who has shown that they can understand a word, to produce that word themselves in speech. This is important when thinking about learning a language. The learner will need great exposure to spoken words before the learning will actually become internalised and produce a result.

So at first the child talks in monosyllabic utterances.

One word sentences.

Indeed often even less than one word! The adult responds by accepting that the child's sound has a shared meaning. This is very exciting, and in fact is really making life easier for child and adult.

Of course, language does not develop in isolation from other development. Parallel to ***language*** development is ***emotional, social, cognitive and physical*** development. Indeed these ingredients of development seem to be ***interdependent*** in their growth.

These are very big words to use when referring to a small child producing very simple recognisable sounds like mama, dada. But if you stop and really think about it, they cannot speak a word without each of these 'ingredients' being present. Language does not develop in a vacuum or independently of other skills.

Every new experience provokes the new vocabulary to absorb it. Very often with the young child this is shown most clearly in play.

Especially role play.

For instance, the adult may be assigned a role, as in 'You be the lady who wants to buy things, and I'll be the checkout lady.' Or 'You be the doctor and I'm the mummy bringing my baby for medicine.' Or they have long conversations on a toy or 'pretend' phone.

The child is not only exploring what it feels like to be another character but is also learning and reinforcing the language to go with the role.

At 3.4 Erin started at kindergarten. By 3.5 her vocabulary included items like, 'Line up!', 'house points' 'register' and so on. This was certainly not language acquired at home.

We had an insight into the daily procedures in the nursery from seeing her play with her dolls and teddies, assigning them roles in her new position as teacher. To hear her saying, '*Do* stop crying teddy!' gave us a good idea of the language mode of staff. This was definitely a nursery item, as we would use a different form of words to a crying child.

How had this development in Erin's language from her earlier 'bay, bah, boh' matured so rapidly that now she could import new terminology so easily back to her home?

The stages in early child development been well charted by researchers in the field.

The actual sequence of language learning in the first year goes something like this:-

The infant cries to signal needs, but cooing and babbling emerge when the child is more contented. He listens to 'motherese', and gradually the babbling becomes more refined and the first recognisable words are said. These seem to be almost the same worldwide. A consonant and vowel combined to make 'mama', 'baba', 'dada', 'bye bye'' and so on.

That is the sequence of development put very simply.

However extraordinarily detailed research has been done on the early milestones of human language learning. And a look at these may show more insight into the *whole* human learning process.

Berry (1969) made a description of language development in children from the first month to the third year of life. He also describes the steps in the development of non verbal behaviour up to the age of 16 months.

Equally Lenneberg (1966) provided a remarkably detailed account of the correlation that exists between the physical, cognitive and linguistic milestones in a child's development.

Later Bruner studied baby's language by videoing infants at home with their mothers. All of this type of research, and much more like it, throw great light on the beginnings of speech and communication.

In the following chapters there is a brief summary of the earliest steps on the way to speech. Age is indicated in months and years. For example 0.9 means 9 months, or 2.3 means 2 years and 3 months. And so on.

All are average milestones and some babies will get there quicker than others, some slower. But all will follow the same *sequence* of acquisition.

That is to say, the *order* in which the development occurs doesn't vary much from child to child.

That order was a key concept in language acquisition for a child is known from the work of Roger Brown. In 1973 he published the findings of his research team. They had intensively studied three toddlers, Eve, Adam and Sarah, for nearly two years. One result of this study was to show that the amazingly sudden speed of language acquisition starts at different times for different toddlers. While Adam and Sarah were both nearly two and a half before they spoke in comprehensible two word sentences, Eve did the same at just twenty months!

But all three followed a similar *progression* in their development of learning to speak.

So the time at which any particular item is acquired can vary enormously, even within the development of children from the same family.

For instance, my first child didn't walk or talk until very late if compared to the second who was about six months ahead of him in both stages. Maybe because she had a model and he didn't; maybe because, as is sometimes noted, girls are ahead of boys in acquiring language.

Chapter Seven

Stages of Language Development In An Infant

Ages 0.0 to 0.5
The main job an infant has to do in the first year of his life is twofold.

Firstly, he must learn to control the muscles he needs to operate precisely for speech production.

Secondly, he must be able to identify the particular sounds, or 'phonetic distinctions' which belong in his mother tongue.

These sounds are called phonemes.

A phoneme is a separate or distinct unit of a language which corresponds to a separate or distinct unit of speech sound. It is the smallest possible meaningful segment of language. For example, to be able to say 'cat' the infant must have control over the phonemes, 'kuh,', 'aah' and 'tuh.'

So when we hear babies babbling, crooning, gurgling and so on, they are in effect tuning up their speech production abilities – in fact working extremely hard! – to have the basics ready to understand, learn and produce the words used in their mother tongue. (Kuhl, et al 1992.)

Age 0.1
At this early stage the infant responds to sound. In particular he appears pleased to hear his mother's voice. He can cry in varying pitches, depending on what he is crying for, or for how long.

Stages of Language Development In An Infant

The child will often stop crying when he hears a familiar friendly voice, and though arm and leg movements are still reflexes rather than directed movements, the baby may even move arms or legs 'in response' to the voice. He will not move when 'listening', but wriggle or move limbs a lot when 'replying'.

Even this early stage is significant in the child's developing language. He vocalises and gets a response!

To ignore an infant's cries is to say that vocalisations don't work. He needs a listener if he is to learn a language. But if his cries *are* answered then he slowly begins to realise how he can influence those around him. Make a noise!

This is his first real understanding of 'cause and effect'!

Age 0.2

Continues to vocalise, and when fully awake he will now smile to show a response to friendly tones of voice.

His own sound production is very limited. It consists of 'ah' when he is very alert and interacting with his minder. This will often result in the minder 'replying' with an encouraging 'ah' to persuade the infant to continue. If he does 'reply' the minder will quite frequently draw the attention of others to this saying something like, 'Did you hear that? He answered me! He is trying to talk!' In addition there is a closed mouth kind of 'nnn' sound when he has had enough of 'ah' and is drawing attention to the fact that he is tired or hungry.

This adult interpretation of infant sound is a major key in language acquisition.

By interpreting the sounds as speech the adult shows the child the essential basics of using these sounds as a means of communication.

Age 0.3

By three months a child is aware of auditory and visual stimuli in his environment. He is able to vocalise his feelings appropriately, gurgling when happy and contented; or grizzling when in need of a nappy change, hungry or lonely.

Parents quickly learn to decipher which cry is which. Again it is the outside interpretation which validates the sound as having meaning. And it is adult response which decides much of the fate of the child's earliest understanding of language. By endorsing the sounds as having meaning, (i.e. this cry means that he is hungry; that cry means that he is thirsty) adults reinforce the child's ability, and desire to communicate.

The Language Barrier

Some people say that responding quickly to a child's cry will spoil the child, and consequently, ultimately make life miserable for both child and adult. This may be true for an older child but certainly not at this early stage where it is a vital part of reinforcing the child's understanding of sound used as a means of communication.

Age 0.4

At four months he can use some simple sign language. For example he can raise his arms when he wants to be picked up. He is able to turn his head in the direction of a voice or other noise.

The babbling continues but now there may be longer stretches of sound – 'ba ba,ba ba'. He can manage four or five syllables at a time! He doesn't always need an audience for this babbling, and when fed, dry and comfortable may vocalise away to himself.

Age 0.5

At this stage the infant shows further evidence of the development in his ability to recognise the direction of voices or sounds. This can be recognised by the physical response, the turning of the head, the eye contact, his smiles and so on.

He still babbles.

He now also develops the really amazing ability in one so young to decode the emotional tone of spoken communication. He responds to speech, and cries at an angry sounding voice, and smiles or laughs at a caring or kind tone of voice.

I have to admit that a game I like to play with small babies of this age is to coo gently at them words like, 'Ah! The dirty, naughty little baby! Are you driving me mad with your demands then? Ah! The naughty baby!'

The joke for me is to see the child smiling and gurgling in agreement.

Tone of voice is *everything* as regards meaning to the child at this stage.

This seems to me to be strong evidence for the fact that the emotional state of the learner is integral to language development.

This applies not only to learning language but to any type of learning the future may hold for the infant.

The child who receives positive response will be content and **wish** to learn.

The child who has to demand attention will only learn because he **has** to in order to survive – get a bottle, a nappy change or whatever.

Chapter Eight

A Key Stage In Physical Development Of Speech – The Dropped Epiglottis

A$_{ge}$ 0.6
By this stage in most babies the epiglottis will have dropped. This is a crucial step in being physically able to produce articulate speech.

This evolution in humans which allows clear articulation and distinctness in speech sounds is, for the very young, both a blessing, and at the same time, a possible risk factor. It most often occurs between the third and fifth month of life.

Speech facilitates easier learning, and this learning allows quicker assimilation of knowledge and skills. This in turn promotes faster solutions to problems and makes it easier to adjust to changing situations. This is the good side.

The risk factor in these crucial early months is that unless the musculature of the mouth and throat are developing properly there is a risk of choking for the child.

As adults, there are two ways of getting air into our lungs, through the nose or through the mouth. Infants have no such option. New born babies are what are known as 'obligate' nose breathers. This means that the child has no option except to breathe through its nose. It is 'obliged' to breathe through its nose. An 'obligate' breather'!

Its oral airway is not yet developed enough to allow for frequent breathing through the mouth.

It might interest you to know that about the only time an infant does not breathe through its nose is when it is crying!

Also, this explains why a runny nose cold for a small child is particularly worrisome. Literally the infant's airways are blocked. We all know that air is life. Without it we die. We can survive for quite a while without food or water, but not without air.

Some remarkable research was done by an anatomy professor, Edmund Crelin, at Yale university. He explains the anatomical development of infants as follows.

In a new born infant the relationship between the soft palate at the back of the roof of the mouth and the epiglottis in the throat is uniquely different from that of an adult. When a newborn's mouth is closed during quiet respiration, the epiglottis and soft palate touch.

During breastfeeding, the epiglottis elevates and touches the tip of the soft palate. This movement divides the archway at the back of the mouth (isthmus faucium) into *two* canals, instead of one.

This may sound pretty boring but it is a brilliant piece of human engineering, the result of which is to allow a newborn to breathe <u>and</u> swallow at the same time. Adults cannot do this. In the adult the function of the epiglottis – a small tissue flap at the base of the tongue – is to cover the larynx during swallowing to prevent solids or liquid being dropped into the lungs.

The reason that a child can breathe and swallow at the same time is that the neuromuscular pathways in their mouths and throats have not yet fully developed.

Breastfeeding can develop these neuromuscular pathways.

Why is this?

At birth, the tongue's natural position is in an advanced forward position. The tongue extends over the lower gum to protect the mother's breast when the child is feeding.

The coordinated effort of all the mouth, jaw, and facial muscles which takes place during breastfeeding assures proper development of all these muscles. When sufficiently mature the epiglottis drops and the tongue is pulled back into the mouth. One third of the tongue, which had previously *all* been in the mouth cavity, is drawn back as well at this time. This one third of the tongue will now become the front wall of the part of the throat at the back of the mouth.

After the epiglottis drops it never comes as near to the soft palate again as it did in infancy. Adults can then no longer breathe and swallow

A Key Stage In Physical Development Of Speech

at the same time but they *do* now have the ability to breathe through their mouth in the event of the nasal airways being blocked.

Of all mammal species on earth only humans have this unique characteristic – the dropped epiglottis. This is why we are capable of all the nuances and variations in the spoken sounds of the world's languages.

The ancient myths of language in different cultures give an indication of some vestiges of memory of the time this amazing evolution in human biology must have occurred.

For example, the United States Wishram Indians believe that the language spoken by them is a *second* language to the tribe.

The first language is that used by babies, dogs, coyotes and shamans, that is, those who are believed to be capable of communicating with the spirit world. Perhaps Wishram first language means the powerful unspoken communication which occurs when there is silence.

Many of the Indians of the Great Plains had similar beliefs.

Cheyenne teaching says:-

'Long ago, men and animals and spirits all communicated in the same way. Then something happened. After that, men had to speak to each other in different languages. But they retained "The Old Language" in dreams, and for communicating with spirits and animals and plants.'

Or again, this power of spoken language is impressively described in a traditional Eskimo poem, called 'Magic Words.'

> In the very earliest of time
> When both people and animals lived on earth
> A person could become an animal if he wanted to,
> an animal could become a human being.
> Sometimes they were people
> And sometimes animals
> And there was no difference.
> All spoke the same language.
> That was the time when words were like magic.
> The human mind had mysterious powers.
> A word spoken by chance
> Might have strange consequences.
> It would suddenly come alive
> And what people wanted to happen would happen.
> All you had to do was say it.
> Nobody could explain this.
> That's the way it was.

The Language Barrier

(Taken from J. Rothenberg's Shaking The Pumpkin – a collection of Amerindian literature.)

Maybe this first language is kinaesthetic; that which, perhaps, today we would define as sign language.

This communication seems to have been completely through body language, the lift of an eyebrow, the shrug of a shoulder, the movement of the hands and so on. It would be the basis of ritual, dance, art, music and drama.

The old language would be thoughts as images rather than words. And communication would be by gesture and body language.

After all at six months the child can distinguish between friendly and angry talk and react appropriately. That is, even at this early stage, emotion, physical response, as well as cognition are involved in the process of developing speech.

In looking at the pattern of development of speech in very young children it becomes clearer that these ancient legends of language are true at a very deep level of knowing things.

There was a time when humans had no spoken language. They communicated with gesture and sign, just as infants do nowadays. Later human speech as we know it developed, but humans at some profoundly basic level of thought have not forgotten other means of communication. We tend to pay attention to the most conscious level, but the deeper, older means are still available to us if we choose to use them.

In one sense we are ourselves occasionally made aware of this.

You know the kind of situation where you say, 'I know this to be true but it seems to me that….' and here you state what factor is clashing with your purely cognitive perception of something. In the above type of statement the 'I' and the 'me' in the sentence are at loggerheads! You can demonstrate this most easily with optical illusions. 'I know that both lines are straight but it seems to me that they are curved!'

Or indeed it can happen in real life. One night my daughter's dog started barking. Her husband called to the animal to shut up the racket and then tried to return to sleep. My daughter however decided that there was an urgency about the animal's noise which required further investigation.

'I know he can bark at nothing when he's in the mood, and I don't fancy going downstairs, but it seems to me that I should.'

Here again the clash between surface logic and a deeper feeling of knowingness.

A Key Stage In Physical Development Of Speech

Accordingly she went to see why he was so upset. Huge flames were leaping into the air from an industrial building which backed unto her garden!

Good thing the dog *told* her what was happening!

Not in so many words, I agree, but **by getting her to pay attention to what was attracting his own attention so closely.**

There is very rigorously conducted research to show that a really helpful thing for parents to do for their children aged between 8 and 12 months is to encourage them to point. This is because pointing is linked closely to **the act of paying joint attention to something,** to object naming by the parent, and language acquisition by the child.

Chapter Nine

The Earliest Speech Sounds

A_{ge} 0.7

The child pays attention to the speech of persons around him and his family members. He listens to his own private vocalizations, and he now enjoys imitating sound sequences. He is able to vocalize emotional satisfaction or dissatisfaction, by sound if not by words.

He begins babbling and pays attention to the sounds of voices.

Some speech like sounds may appear. These seem to be universally 'mama, baba, dada'.

These sounds are merely noise from the throat – the 'aaah!' – made when making no attempt at speech, merely making sound. It is the most relaxed speech sound ever! If the lips happen to be closed when saying 'aah' the sound that emerges is 'baba.' If the child is wailing, the lips drawn back, – go on pretend to wail and see what happens! – the sound is 'mama'! If the child has its tongue in a sucking position the sound is 'dada'.

Now I don't believe that the child is talking as such at this stage.

But I do believe that in accepting the sounds as vocal communication – apparently naming his parents and himself – the parents encourage further production of these sounds. If baby sees people around him happy to hear him say, 'mama, baba, dada,' then to ensure this attention he will strive to repeat the process, and gradually gain more physical control of the means of speech production.

But the real key to this breakthrough lies more with his minders than himself. By accepting his sounds as comprehensible meaning they have provided the incentive to speak. In getting almost involuntary sounds under control he is also discovering the key to future word production as a part of communication.

And notice that even at this early stage language does not develop in isolation from other forms of development; namely:-

physical (to control mouth and throat movement),

cognitive (to understand that control is needed and know that particular sounds get an approval response),

emotional, (to want to please and be pleased), and finally

social (only as part of a group can he communicate wants, needs, feelings, and be understood).

Age 0.8

He begins to be alert to all stimuli in the immediate environment. He will notice the wind moving branches, the presence of a family pet, the television, and so on.

On the production side, back vowels, that is those articulated near the back of the vocal cavity, begin to sound more like speech sounds.

He vocalizes syllables, interjections and expresses recognition. Above all he copies the intonation of things he hears around him.

Age 0.9

The child is able to comprehend simple symbolic gestures and intonation patterns. If he is offered a bottle or a toy say, he will reach for it if he wants it. He will point to objects that interest him and indicate that he wants them. Equally he is capable of rejecting unwanted offers by body language. For example spoon feeding has probably started by now. Parents all know the way a child will compress his lips and turn his head aside from the spoon if it is not acceptable. This is distinctly clear communication!

By this age he also understands, 'No!' It is frequently used by his carers, to stop him doing things like eating soap, or pulling the dog's tail, or dropping his toys out of his pram. The accompanying actions of the carer make the meaning of, 'No.' quite clear.

By this stage he can also recognise his own name, and respond to its use. His own utterances have a chain of about 3 or 4 syllables. The frequent copying of intonation patterns continues. He *sounds* like he is talking, even though meaning is not at all clear for a listener.

Echolalia (constant imitation of sounds of the environment) is the chief characteristic of this month. Echolalia is when the child parrot fashion repeats the speech of somebody else. He seems to quite literally echo utterances.

In echolalia, the tone and accent of the speaker is repeated as well.

Facial and arm gestures accompany vocalizations. It is amazing to see such small infants doing things like raising their eyebrows in surprise or enquiry!

Age 0.10

In the tenth month the child exhibits *action* response to *verbal* requests such as 'Where is teddy?'

He can shake or nod his head to express 'yes' or 'no'. The child produces utterances apparently attempting to name objects. The imitation of intonation patterns continues. Many speech sounds are spoken clearly enough to be distinguished, although several non-speech sounds also continue to occur. This is a time of consolidation and extension of communication skills.

Age 0.11

In the eleventh month the child differentiates between family and strangers. There is now every likelihood of the appearance of first words in his speech in this month. Single word utterances begin to emerge. These are often used to indicate his needs or wants. He is beginning to show that he understands words, and around his first birthday may start to produce them himself. (Clark;Ingram)

Age 1.00 to 1.6

Children's first recognisable words are generally agreed to start occurring between 11 and 18 months. Once the child recognises that sound has meaning words start to be acquired at the rate of about three a month. This is in spoken vocabulary; but probably the silent vocabulary is increasing quite dramatically.

These words are spoken in isolation from one another. That is to say they are one word sentences – 'mama, 'teddy,' or 'up.' This one word stage lasts for anything between two months and a year.

The first words of children are remarkably similar all over the world, in children from every type of culture and background.

Roughly half the words *name objects*. They include food, people, body parts, clothes, toys, and household items.

There are words for *actions and routines*, like 'up', out,' and 'go.'

Then there are words for *social interactions*, like 'bye,' 'yes' and 'no.'

The Earliest Speech Sounds

Finally there are a few *chunks of words* such as 'Look at that' or 'What is that?' which are used by the child as if they were one word and not a group of three. Children may vary in how many objects they name, or how much social interaction they use, but nevertheless all children will use both.

Chapter Ten

An Analysis Of The First Fifty Words

We kept a record of Erin's first fifty words. The list was completed when Erin was 17 months old.

We defined words as a clear sound made by her, which we understood. Words which we could see that she recognised, but had not as yet spoken on her own initiative, were not included. That is, we listed words in her 'productive' vocabulary, which means sounds she made which we perceived to have an intended meaning to her.

Equally her words did not have to be spoken completely in standard English. For example, 'chair' is listed because she said 'chay' quite clearly, and obviously *meant* chair. We could see this from her gestures or body language and of course the context. So this was acceptable. She was speaking sounds with intended meaning.

I have included a brief commentary on her range of words which should also be useful to you.

I found it fascinating to record the words as they appeared, and to see the stages they went through before they became standard English.

Research shows that during the second year of talk the average child can manage the consonants

b,f,k,n,p,d,g,m,and h

at the *beginning* of words, but only the first five in the list

b,f,k,n,p.

can be said at the *end* of a word.

You will probably forget this as soon as you read it but never mind. What is important to know is that a single consonant is easier to say than

An Analysis Of The First Fifty Words

a double like 'st' or 'cr''; and that some consonants are easier to say than others.

Erin's individual words show that she pretty much fits the norm here. Initially many words are shortened or altered before developing into standard English. So what starts for example as 'all goh' becomes in time 'all gone'. Similarly longer words may be shortened to facilitate the child's ability to say them. Banana often becomes 'nana', and so on.

Repetition is practised by most children, some to a greater extent than others. They may take the first syllable of a word and repeat it to get across their meaning. For example 'water' may be 'wahwah' at this stage.

First fifty words.

1. Apple
2. Baby
3. Bad
4. Bag
5. Ball
6. Banana
7. Bath
8. Bear
9. Bed
10. Bread
11. Bubble
12. Car
13. Chair
14. Cheese
15. Cheers
16. Chicken
17. Clap
18. Clock
19. Cow
20. Cup of tea
21. Daddy
22. Dog
23. Duck
24. Egg
25. Eye
26. Food
27. Gone
28. Goodbye
29. Grandma

30. Hat
31. Hello
32. Hot
33. I want that
34. Juice
35. Milk
36. More
37. Mummy
38. No
39. Nose
40. Nursery rhymes
41. Out
42. Phaaw!
43. Pillow
44. Plane
45. Shoe
46. Sky
47. Teeth
48. Thank you
49. Teddy
50. Tree

1. 'apple' said quite clearly but in Erin's mind meant any fruit which is not a banana. This is a clear example of overextension. This is when for example a child realises that a male adult in the household is called Daddy. He then over extends the meaning of the word and calls every adult male he sees, 'Daddy'.

I was very interested to see on a television program dealing with the history of the English language that 'apple' was an old English word with roots in Anglo Saxon and old German.

Originally it meant apple and *other fruits besides.*

Then with French speaking invasions of England the French word 'fruits' came into the English language. Now with another word available 'apple' came to be confined to the one fruit we name as such today.

This process in national language acquisition seemed to me to mirror the stages of language acquisition in the individual child.

The process continues today.

When I was a child the first image in my brain for the word 'mouse' was a small scurrying, squeaking little animal. I do think today's child would first visualise the manual control instrument that is used with computers, and then the little living creature. Or perhaps the second 'mouse' image,

An Analysis Of The First Fifty Words

for contemporary children, is to them just the almost imaginary little creature of nursery rhymes and stories; as unlikely as Humpty Dumpty!

2. 'baby' Easy to say with the repetition of the 'b' consonant.

3. 'bad' If she fell or hurt herself, the floor or chair, or whatever she had knocked into, was 'bad'.

So this word is also a vivid reminder of her stage of motor development at this time. She could stand up and walk but as yet had not got full control of the large motor movement required to do so without occasionally tumbling, or knocking into objects in her path. However she was so intoxicated with her new found freedom that a few bumps were ignored, and accepted as part of the price for independence.

4. 'bag' This was pronounced 'bak'.

5. 'ball' Began as 'baw', moved to 'ball'. The acquisition of this word was encouraged by the World Cup football games! At that time her Dad was keenly interested in the matches. He groaned for penalties awarded when he felt them undeserved. 'That was a dive!' Erin learned to hurl herself on the ground when she heard the word 'dive', but it is not included here as she herself never actually *said* 'dive'.

As this was an early word, inevitably I suppose, it reminded me of an incident in my own youngest child's language development. It was one January when he was 15 months old. He had had his first football as a present at Christmas. He really loved it and demanded, 'Fuh baw', at every opportunity. We then had to roll it to him, and he would try to roll or hurl it back. This particular bitterly cold January evening he had been bathed and fed and I was carrying him along the hall to take him upstairs for bed.

He grabbed the outside door handle as we passed, and said, 'Fuh baw!'

'No.' I said, 'It's cold and late and bed time. No football!'

'Fuh baw!', he insisted more adamantly, clinging to the door handle.

'No!' I said equally firmly.

'Fuh baw!' He really yelled it at me.

'What's going on?' called my husband from another room.

I was fed up and tired. I said, 'Right you sort it if you want to. This fellow wants to go out the garden now and play football and there is no way I'm having him get chilled before bedtime. It's freezing out there.'

'Well why don't you open the door and show him that?'

I flung the door wide and stepped out into the icy snow.

The child raised his arm and pointed to where a full moon sailed through the clear sky.

'Fuh baw. Fuh baw!'

A simple overextension of meaning. He must have seen the moon through the kitchen window and had only wished to show it to me.

How many quarrels and disagreements may be nothing but a misinterpretation of meaning?

6. (ba)nana She actually said 'nana'. This was the first fruit to be differentiated from apples.

7. 'bath' This was said, 'bah'.

8. 'bear' pronounced "bay'. Bear was a character in her then favourite children's programme.

9. 'bed' Sometimes 'bet'.

10. 'bread' distinguishable from meaning bed by the context of its usage.

11. 'bubble' Quite clear from the first attempt. Plenty of consonant repetition. And she loves bath time. Also her parents had bought her a bubble machine!

12. 'car' Pronounced 'ka', this sound covered cars, vans, lorries, indeed any road vehicle. This was another example of overextension.

13. 'chair' Said as 'chay'.

14. 'cheese' She said 'chee'.

15. 'cheers' Again she said, 'chee'.

We knew which chee was which by tone of voice and context.

For 'cheese' she either indicated it on the table, or headed for the fridge to get some out for herself.

For 'cheers' she reached out her bottle to clink it with someone's glass. Again notice that for this word she needed to be able to sit up independently, and have the hand and eye coordination necessary to get her bottle to reach the glass she wanted to clink. She understood that on special occasions adults touched glasses like this. This was not everyday mealtime behaviour! Physical, social, cognitive, and language development were going hand in hand.

16. 'chicken' Erin said, 'chika'. This referred to a favourite finger food and not the farm bird.

17. 'clap' Erin actually said, 'cap' to begin with only later getting the 'l' sound in the word. This was probably acquired from the nursery rhyme, "Clap hands, clap hands till Daddy comes home.' She liked at this time rhymes that involved physical involvement, like 'Pat a cake' or 'Round and round the garden'.

18. 'clock' Erin's version of this word was 'cok'. It was used for clock or watch.

An Analysis Of The First Fifty Words

19. 'cow' Holidays in rural Ireland improved Erin's acquaintance with cows. We would know she wanted to walk and see them by her insistent demands of, 'Moo!'

20. 'cup of tea' (said as one word) 'cuppatea' very similar to, but equally quite distinct from, her own invented sound – 'gobbety gobbety' – to mean nursery rhyme book.

21. 'daddy' Consonant repetition.

22. 'dog' She actually said, 'goggy'. Consonant repetition.

23. 'duck' 'kak kak' imitating the noise of the duck. We liked to go and feed some ducks on a nearby canal.

24. 'egg' said as 'ek'.

25. 'eye' meaning a part of the body but occasionally, depending on context, by this sound she meant 'slide'.

26. 'food' This was called 'yum yum' and was obvious from context. This was often accompanied by the gesture of rubbing her hand in a circular movement on her tummy – an early use of sign language!

27. 'gone' Said as 'goh!' This was often accompanied by a fingers spread wide, palms turning back and forth, and arms opening out gesture – another piece of sign language to emphasise her point.

This was also a sign of cognitive development.

Object permanence!

Here we have to move briefly into the world of Jean Piaget, one of the 'household gods' of educational theory.

Piaget was originally a biologist, but his later studies of, and comments on, children's development is where his real reputation lies.

Though it now seems as obvious as the nose on your face he pointed out that as children grow or mature, they are capable of more complicated tasks than those which they could accomplish when younger.

By careful observation and recording he saw that a child's development does not progress in a smooth line. Instead there are certain points at which cognitive learning can take a sudden great leap forward. One of the stages he identified is referred to as the idea of 'object permanence.' That is, when a child usually over eight months of age shows that it knows that teddy or bottle or whatever object still exists even though it cannot be seen or touched.

That is, it has a permanence, or existence, outside of the child's experience of it.

So for Erin to say 'all gone' means she knows that food or drink is no longer here, and that it was here at some other time.

28. 'goodbye'. Pronounced as 'bye bye'.

29. 'Grandma' She called me 'mama,' 'Grandma' was far too much to attempt so eventually Erin took the last consonant and vowel sound and used the trick of repetition and intonation to get a clear meaning across. The second 'ma' was far more forceful than the first.

Another grandchild took different action with the same word. Her mother referred to me as Granny so the child initially addressed me as 'Danny'. The consonant cluster 'gr' was abandoned and the easier 'd' substituted. Again note the easy vowel 'a' and the repetition of sound.

30. 'hat' This was one of her later words in the fifty, and was correctly said from the start.

31. 'hello' Moved from 'lo' to 'ello'. Used only when she was on her play phone. That is, she initially did not greet people with 'hello'. At first it was to her what you said before you could talk on the phone. The initial 'hello' was always followed by a flood of speech often mostly incomprehensible to anyone except the child herself, but with pauses, as in any conversation. 'Play' telephone calls always ended with a cheery, 'bye bye'.

32. 'hot' Pronounced, 'hoh'.

Always accompanied by exaggerated blowing on hot food, or pulling her hands back dramatically from the source of heat, and holding them to her chest in an overacted protective movement.

33. 'I want that/give me that.'

To get this meaning across Erin used body language and said, 'uh uh.'

It was one of her earliest meaningful utterances, used with gestures and pointing to indicate what she wanted. When later 'uh! uh!' was used by her mother in a deliberate role reversal mood, to get Erin to crawl and fetch toys from the floor for *her* they both enjoyed the game very much.

Despite this 'uh uh' quite quickly disappeared, perhaps because the child was more mobile and able to crawl or later walk, to get what she wanted for herself.

34. 'juice' She actually said, 'chuse'.

36. 'more' This was said as 'mo'.
37. 'Mummy' more often 'mum.'
38. 'No' This word was perfectly clear, both in sound and meaning, from the start.
39. 'nose' Progressed from the sound 'no' to 'nose'.
40. Nursery Rhymes She called her rhymes book 'gobbety gobbety'.

An Analysis Of The First Fifty Words

Erin really enjoyed listening to nursery rhymes and had her favourite book. Perhaps the rhyme, rhythm and repetition of verses like 'hickory dickory dock' or 'To market to market to buy a fat hen' inspired this piece of really creative speech! To make perfectly sure it was the nursery rhymes book she meant by 'gobbety gobbety' one day I pretended that I couldn't see it. Erin looked herself, found it and gave it to me, saying with great satisfaction, 'gobbetty gobbetty mama!'

41. 'out' (spoken as a command to the dog to leave the room).

Speaking to the dog she also pointed to the door when giving her command to him. Later she developed it to mean, 'Get me out of my pushchair/high chair I want to walk!' This second 'out' was accompanied by shifting in her seat and raising her hands in the air.

42. 'Phaaw!'

Bad smells evoked a very dramatic 'phaaw' with waving hand in front of her face gestures.

This is an example of interjectional speech. This is sometimes referred to as a 'filled pause.' It is a completely natural and spontaneous exclamation, usually accompanied by gestures, facial expressions and gesticulations. The speaker moves his hands and arms to emphasise the extent of feeling.

Interjections usually have no grammatical connection to the rest of the sentence and simply express an emotion or an attitude on the part of the speaker, although most interjections have clear definitions. They are used when the speaker encounters situations which cause these emotions – unexpectedly, painfully, surprisingly or in any other sudden way. Here are some common interjections

Sh!
Ugh!
Oh!

In more advanced speech expletives may be regarded as interjections. The rude word which escapes the mouth when, say, we drop something, or when driving ourselves another driver behaves dangerously badly. They verbally express the immediate emotional response to the situation.

Erin's 'Phaaw!' was slightly different as she more often used it to joke, for instance carrying her dad's shoes to the hall. She would giggle happily saying, 'Phwaaw!' And she used it in role play with her dolls when there was certainly no unpleasant odour.

43. 'Pillow' Like 'bubble' this word came complete.
44. 'Plane' 'pay' to 'pane' to 'plane'.
45. 'Shoe' Spoken clearly quite early.

46. 'sky' This was pronounced 'ki'.
47. 'Teeth' The final 'th' sound took a good while after 17 months of age to appear.
48. 'Teddy' Spoken clearly from the beginning.
49. 'Thank you.' Spoken as 'coo'. Context made the meaning clear.
50. 'Tree' pronounced 'tee'.

Chapter Eleven

Towards Clearer Understanding

Now although we accepted the meanings behind some of the half spoken words in the last chapter we all nevertheless agreed on a strategy to help Erin towards standard pronunciation. When she used her version of a word we were careful to use the same word, but correctly pronounced, in our response to her.

Take 'tee' for teeth. If she was in the bathroom and asking in her one word way to clean her 'tee' by pointing to them and reaching for her brush we would describe the situation to her. 'Are you getting your brush to clean your *teeth*? Let me see your nice *teeth*. Here's the brush for your *teeth* and now you need paste for your *teeth*.' And so on. By this sort of action though we were not directly correcting her pronunciation we were at least offering her a model of how it should be.

Now for some other useful points about words in this list.

When two or more consonants occur in a word together like 'cl' and 'ck' in 'clock', 'sk' in 'rusk', or 'Chr ' and 'stm' in' Christmas', this is called a *consonant cluster.*

Children starting to speak tend to avoid these consonant clusters. The reason for this is fairly obvious. They are harder to say than single consonants. Try it yourself and see.

Stop and consciously note the lack of effort needed to say 'a' as in 'baby'; now
    try 'baby' itself.

Next, slowly feel what you do to say 'gr' in grandma. You need much more control of your mouth and tongue.

43

The Language Barrier

Some of you might remember a young child talking about 'Kismas'. Now you know it's those consonant clusters which make Christmas so hard to say!

Children use all kinds of clever tactics to overcome sounds which are, for the moment, difficult to say accurately. Dropping part of the cluster is one.

Erin did this quite frequently in her earlier acquisition of words. She would 'keen' her teeth, or ask for 'mik' meaning milk.

One technique used by Erin to avoid attempting to say a word – 'Horse' – caused us amusement while it lasted.

We have a friend, Susie, whose daughter is called Ellie. Both names are easy for a beginner to say having easy vowel sounds and repetition of sounds. But her husband was known to everyone as Horse.

Erin at 25 months found this word was beyond her.

So when asked, 'Who are we going to see?' she would reply, 'Susie, Ellie, and …..' she would then make a clicking noise with her tongue to the roof of her mouth to imitate the sound of a horses hooves clattering on a road. She had learned this clip clop 'horse' sound from us when we were playing with her riding on her rocking horse.

Another tactic she used for the same purpose of avoiding difficult pronunciation occurred later in her life. At 3.3 she was on the phone to her mother.

She was explaining what she was doing. [Peeling hard boiled eggs.]

'Mum it's very difficu', very difficu'.

She abandoned difficult.

'Mum it's very hard work!'

In her first 50 words you can see reductions occurring quite often. For example, she reduced 'sky' to 'ki', and 'clap' to 'cap'. She finally got 'plane', but went to the accurate pronunciation in stages. And, for her, possibly the word was of big significance, as she had recently gone on holiday with her parents to see her grandad in India and clocked up six flights in the process. So she must have heard the word plane frequently, and also she had the first hand experience of being on one.

The other consonant cluster she manages is 'sh' in 'shoe'. This word is frequently in the first fifty words of a child when a list is kept, so it seems fairly easy for an under two, probably because it is mostly made by simply expelling air from the mouth.

(Or on a lighter note maybe because from the day they are born the babies are listening to someone saying, 'Shh! Don't wake the baby!', when they are supposed to be asleep, or, 'Shh!' to them if they are awake and crying.)

Erin also used the consonant cluster 'ch' in 'cheese' and 'cheers'. From getting the 'sh' sound it may be fairly easy to get the 'ch' sound.

I also wonder whether the emergence of teeth in the mouth enables a child to cope better with enunciating some sounds. The letter 's' for example must be nearly impossible for a toothless infant.

We talk about the mumbling elderly.

Like infants they are minus their teeth!

Also vowels are interesting. She could get the sound of 'u' as in 'cup' and 'up' quite early on. But the initial 'u' sound as in 'uniform' and 'Eugene' was even at 3.5 an 'oo' as in 'moon' sound.

At the early stages of language acquisition, when the child is aged somewhere between 1.00 and 1.06 he relies on expression, gesture and intonation to make even one word do a lot of work. An example of this to illustrate what I mean.

I was minding Erin while her mother was out shopping. Erin was 14 months at the time.

We both heard someone at the front door.

Erin cocked her head to one side in a listening pose and said to me, 'Mummy?' I said, 'Maybe. Let's see.' Then we heard her mother's voice speaking to the dog. Erin said in a very pleased tone of voice, 'Mummy'. She then raised her voice and called loudly, 'Mummy!' I think that this ability of very young children to use the one word as:-

1. Question – Is that my mum at the door?
2. Statement – Yes. It is my mum.
3. Imperative demand – Mum, come here!
– is little short of genius!

It means that a minimal vocabulary can go a very long way.

These one word sentences are most common in the early days of speech. But again notice that the child relies on the adult to interpret precisely *which* meaning the child intended.

From this stage on it is more difficult to generalise about children's language development in detail as each child is the product of a unique environment, where all kinds of outside factors will affect the progress made by each individual learner. Studies at the University of Kansas now show that the more language a child listens to in these early days the more he will learn. Not only will his ability to talk improve but also his thinking processes.

The studies also show that the child who gets positive responses to his attempts at conversation, scores far higher on I.Q. tests than those who don't receive such regular daily feedback.

Their research indicates that parents should try to use all kinds of talk around a child. You don't have to do much 'motherese' once words start appearing.

On the contrary there is evidence that the more fully you speak to a child, and respond to him the greater his capacity for both language and thought.

Most small children seem to go through a phase where they wear out every adult around them by their persistent questioning!

So for example a child may point out a flower and say, 'What's that?'

Now you could answer, 'A flower.'

Or you could say, 'That's a flower. There are all kinds of flowers. This flower is a rose. Roses are very pretty flowers. Shall we look for some more flowers in the garden?'

In either case the most immediate response you may get from the child may be the word, 'Fahwah!'; but the *second* type of reply has been scientifically verified as the type which develops more fluent language development and higher intellectual performance in children.

The difference between the first adult reply and the second, is in the *quality* of the conversational exchange. As a matter of fact the factors which signify the highest quality in such exchanges have been identified as follows.

1. The first and most important is quite simply an *awareness* on the part of the adult that language is important. The world is named and explained for the child, who often appears neither to care, nor even yet to understand. He is just focussed on securing a caring adult's attention!

2. The adults gave more *affirmative feedback* to the child. They frequently said things like, 'Yes.' That's right.' 'Good.' and other similar phrases.

3. They used a *variety of vocabulary* of all types. They used a range of verbs, nouns, adjectives and adverbs.

4. The adults asked lots of front ended, open, descriptive yes/no *questions*. 'Do you think we could…..?' etc.

5. They used very *few imperatives* – 'Do this' – and far *fewer prohibitive statements* – 'No!', 'Don't.', 'Stop!'

These are very simple ideas and easily incorporated in to any adult's language usage when dealing with children. There is no rocket science here.

Yet it constantly amazes me how many carers, both those in charge of under fives, and teachers of older children in schools completely ignore much of this carefully researched data; and then wonder why the children are not learning!

In the first pointer above, I wrote that 'The world is named and explained for the child.'

Humans through language name things in their environment in order to classify and categorise them.

They need language to identify the components of the world in a communicable manner. But first children need to find out what these components are.

They do much of this through what we call play. They see, touch, and taste to gain understanding. Without this initial exploration through the senses how can they ever understand the multiplicity of words we use in everyday speech? Words like heavy, light, sad, happy, rough, smooth, wet, dry, – a huge number of words are needed to describe the world around them.

They have to *experience* it before they can verbalise it.

The child needs direct interaction with his world to learn about it. He needs for example to *see* colours – green, blue, yellow, black, – before he can name them. He needs to see and experience tables, chairs, clothes, floors, walls, anything you care to name, before he can understand them.

As the great German educationalist, Friedrich Froebel put it,

"Children must master the language of ***things*** before they master the language of ***words***."

The italics are mine.

This one sentence describes the fundamental nature, the quintessence, of early childhood education. It is the guiding principle behind Froebel's beliefs which led him to start up the creation of kindergartens for pre school children.

Just in large scale movement alone he has to experience sitting, crawling, standing, walking, running, falling, skipping, hopping, dancing, before he can really talk about these things.

Every ordinary experience, walking on grass, feeling the wind or the rain is a huge learning experience. Planting seeds, watering them, seeing a plant grow, seeing falling leaves in Autumn – everything in his environment is part of a hugely time consuming and strenuous process which absorbs all of his energies, and cannot be hurried. Not only has to experience this world around him but he also has to learn the words to explain and describe it.

The more you consider what a child has to experience before he can talk the more awesome the task becomes. If you don't yet think so stop and consider.

How would you design a learning program which would cover everything a child should understand how to do and describe by the time he is age five? What lesson plan would you have for each day? How would you implement your lesson plans?

Yet with no formal teaching, no set curriculum, no timetable, his learning has been prodigious!

Then he starts school.

If the teaching style of the school differs too much from that of the home then the rate of learning will slow dramatically. Fortunately today most nurseries or kindergartens and reception classes are learning the lessons of earliest childhood 'hands on experience' as the great educating force it is.

There are always exceptions of course. Like a head teacher I heard in a radio interview. She was laughing at every parent's belief in the intelligence of their own child. She said every parent she spoke with believed their own child to be very clever, and (here she really was amused) responded well to approachable and kindly treatment. 'They are all sensitive little plants to their parents!' she laughed. 'However there are some real little savages when we get to know them here!' she explained.

I thought no wonder. If you expect them to be so, and treat them like untamed little beasts then what do you expect? Has it never struck you that all of these parents with the same point of view on education – that is that kindness and sensitivity work – might actually be right in their assessments?

Chapter Twelve

The Naming Explosion

Age 1.00–1.6
For some reason, when children have learned about 25 spoken words of vocabulary something quite dramatic happens.

This is called the 'naming explosion' by linguists.

It seems that once a basic critical number of words can be said, a child can add between 10 and 20 new words a week. The variation in the number of words will depend on a number of factors, but significant here will be the quality and quantity of language the child will hears spoken around him, and the amount of listening to he gets.

In my opinion I think the language explosion occurs for two reasons.

1. The child now fully realises that words <u>work</u>. Voice sounds can be controlled to have meaning. They can be used to get him more easily what he wants. To say 'bottle' and get a bottle is far better than shouting with hunger!

2. The child has built up a set of consonant and vowel sounds he knows how to make. He maximises these to pick up new words. For example, Erin could say 'cap' (meaning clap) ; she could also say 'up', wanting to be lifted up. So she had the skills of making the word 'cup', without as much effort and practise as the original two words took her.

I think that this kind of *synthesising* of information and skills – both cognitive and physical – goes on all the time in humans.

We never, or rarely, are aware of the sequences of the learned moves we make daily. Once we have struggled to learn them, and they are known they become part of that great region in the brain called "Things I can do; *without having consciously to think about it.*'

If this is sounding too airy fairy let me give you an example.

A few minutes ago the phone rang. It was a call from my daughter to say that she had left her keys here. Could she pop back and pick them up? Of course she could.

A very simple everyday occurrence – answering a phone.

But stop for a minute and think.

The phone here rings. I answer it.

I listen, speak, hang up.

Sounds simple enough. But I have to have learned at some time the sound a phone makes. I have to know that I must reach it and pick it up and place it to my ear. For the child learner this is the result of a complex series of acquired *physical* and *cognitive* skills. How to hold a phone, which button to press to get a connection to the caller, which end to speak into, where to listen.

I don't even think about it because my mind is focussed on wondering who is phoning and why?

I have to give the conventional for the U.K. greeting, 'Hello.' I understand the *social* norms of where I live. This is a private call, so the caller should recognise my voice and an introduction is unnecessary. There are different formulas for answering the phone.

When I am in the office my response is very different. I give a more formal greeting, such as, 'Good morning.' Then the company name, followed by, 'How can I help you?'

I never really think about this. I am almost on auto pilot!

I have to listen, recognise that this is either a familiar or an unknown voice, and decode the message. I have to use *language* skills. How many brain signals are involved here? Back and forth sweep the messages and responses. Without me being consciously aware of them.

Who is it? Check in my brain voice intonations memory store.

Sarah.

What does her tone of voice indicate? Check brain storage of information on level of emotion carried by tone of voice. *Emotional* content decoding skills.

She sounds O.K.

What do her words mean? Language skills.

This one simple short phone call has involved a multiplicity of skills all so coordinated and easily performed that the mind being focussed on other matters is almost unaware of their operation.

This strikes me as very similar to what I believe are called macros in computers.

As I understand it there is a system, or method, used on computers called a macro, which when you give the machine one command, automatically triggers a number of other subsidiary commands.

This series of subsidiary integrated commands are triggered into action by the one overall command.

So the concept of the macro is very simple. It is *a collection of commands* which, when the macro is activated, causes that *collection of commands* to be executed. This alone is a powerful thing; but its power is vastly increased when "parameter substitution" is performed.

That is when the subsidiary commands are programmed to operate within given situations *with similar characteristics.*

It does not have to be exactly the same situation as the original one, it just needs to have certain characteristics in common.

Say you learn to drive in one kind of car. You can then fairly easily drive *any* kind of car after that because you have 'macroed' the skills to do so. Or say, that using, if I may call it, a 'human macro' to answer one type of phone at home, it should be possible to activate a similar collection of subsidiary commands to answer a slightly different model of phone elsewhere.

With the range of phones now on the market for example, I can't be the only person who has asked, or been asked, 'Which is the "On" button on this?' Beyond that you know everything you need to know. You don't then ask, 'How do I dial?' You are able to get on with your phone call – the whole object of the exercise.

Similarly if you want to use your car to go somewhere, you will use a 'driving macro.' That is to say when you get in your car, (provided you have been a driver for some length of time!) you are more focussed on the purpose of your trip than in thinking, 'I must put the key in the ignition, switch on the engine, etc. etc.' The driving of the car becomes the collection of subsidiary commands to the macro – the object of the outing.

With computers, the primary, overriding purpose in applying macros is to reduce repetition. The advice to pc users is that whenever you find that you have to repeat a certain sequence of commands several times, it is almost always better to construct a macro which contains the sequence, and then execute the macro. It is not only useful to computer users but on reflection it would appear that humans have macros too! The only thing is that once in place we seem to be for the most part unaware of their operating.

This may be because of the structure of the brain.

A variety of techniques have been used by researchers to find out where different functions are located in the brain. Initially this type of research had to depend on studying the effects of physical damage – for example a car accident – on particular parts of the brain. Researchers would then observe what precise effect this damage was having on the patient's physical and mental skills.

Relationships were deduced between the exact location of the damage and the type of impairment the patient then suffered. For example, it was learned that in adults, aphasia (a disorder of the central nervous system characterised by partial or total loss of the ability to communicate, especially in speech or writing) is nearly always the result of injury to the *left* hemisphere.

In one study 97% of 205 aphasics studied had left hemisphere damage.

This type of study is still ongoing, but in addition research into which side of the brain controls different types of operation have been investigated using techniques designed to study the undamaged brain.

In one extremely interesting newspaper report I read of a waiter in Italy who was knocked down in road accident. On regaining consciousness in hospital he was fully aware of who he was, where he worked and where he lived, but was completely unable to name himself, or name any of the persons or places he knew.

All *names* had been completely wiped from his memory.

Doctors were able to trace the very tiny damage done to his brain and thus not only locate where in the brain names were stored, but also deduce that the storage of names was confined to this one tiny area of the brain, separate to all the other information he had about friends and relatives and places.

While researchers continue to rely on data from brain damage, undamaged subjects have also been investigated using several harmless techniques.

For instance, in dichotic listening, subjects are presented with 'competing, simultaneous auditory stimuli '. This quite simply means that at exactly the same instant a sound is fed into the right ear, a slightly similar but different sound is fed into the left. Whichever sound is recorded by the brain as having been heard is thought to lead to the dominant side of the brain for the function of understanding language.

In adults the results of these experiments show a statistically significant right ear advantage for verbal stimuli; and equally interesting, a left ear advantage for musical chords or environmental stimuli.

So using evidence such as this it is now well established that for most people the two sides of the brain perform different functions.

The left hemisphere is responsible for most adult linguistic performance. Recent studies also suggest that the left side is also involved in functions related to the perception of time. The left side of the brain is more efficient than the right in judging the order in time in which sounds occur.

The right hemisphere seems to have the function of Gestalt perception. Gestalt refers to the ability to see the whole of something, its totality, rather than break it down into its component parts and itemise each bit separately. Seeing a picture of a house, we don't say, 'That is a picture of a building with one door and four windows, and a tile roof' or whatever. We say 'That's a house!'

Or looking at a piece of a picture which shows an arc we are able to conclude that the full picture is a circle. Shown part of a portrait we can deduce what the rest of the picture is probably like. This is Gestalt perception.

And even though it is the left side which tends to perceive musical notes most effectively certain aspects of musical perception are now known to be performed by the right hemisphere. While the left is hearing individual notes and timing, the right gains an understanding of the complete piece.

An eminent neurosurgeon, Joseph Bogen, has speculated that the two sides of the brain utilize two different cognitive modes. Only the intactness of the fibres connecting the two hemispheres, gives us the illusion that we have just one mind.

In a similar conclusion, the neuroscientist Karl Pribram put forward a holographic theory of reality. At about just the same time a physicist David Bohm advanced the same notion. Though from different scientific backgrounds they have since both worked together in developing this idea.

Their holographic theory points to a multiplying, rather than adding, effect between the two halves of the brain.

On a very simple level it is rather like getting stereophonic sound. To do so, the left and right output channels must be both properly connected so that they synthesise the sound heard.

But the stereo is just two streams of sound *added* together.

This would be the brain if the two halves were not connected to one another, as would happen if the connections between the two halves were severed. But of course they are both connected and interconnected and the result is that information, perception and cognition are ***multiplied*** by each other and not added to one another. No wonder children can learn to speak with such apparent speed and ease!

Chapter Thirteen

Why It Is Difficult To Program A Computer To Speak Realistically

Possibly without really realising it humans often use analogy, simile or metaphor when teaching a child.

Speaking mathematically an analogy would be saying that 'a is to b as c is to d.'

That is a has a relationship to b which is similar to the relationship c has to d. Expressed linguistically, if you can put in the missing word here you understand analogy:-

Hand is to glove as foot is to …..?

Analogy is a very powerful way of deducing or inferring information. Successful use of analogy helps you explain things, by comparing them closely with things your listener already knows about.

Parents use it all the time to respond to children's questions.

If you say something like, 'That man *is a pig*!' you are using metaphor.

If you say 'He acts *like a pig*!' you are using simile.

Obviously in neither case do you literally mean that the man is an animal. You are more likely saying he has the perceived attributes of a pig – he is greedy, rude and dirty.

Or you might say, 'He is on an emotional roller coaster until he hears the results.'

You certainly don't mean that he is spending all his time on a theme park ride which is likely to burst into alternate tears or laughter!

The Language Barrier

We all use analogy on a daily basis even if we do not ever realise it. And, most importantly, you can compare something your listener doesn't understand, and compare it with something they do, in order to give them a clear path toward understanding your proposition.

Many young children's questions are answered in this way. When as yet they have no experience of something, we look for something similar that they have experienced to help them to get some idea of an answer.

Now analogy is very difficult for computers as there is a very complicated mapping between things that appear to have no relationship at all. The program needs the key property of an object to be able to pick out the analogy.

It needs to know, say, the accepted mannerisms of a pig as in the example above.

If a computer cannot grasp the concept of analogies then it will never be able to talk or answer realistically. This is an important difference between the computer brain – which follows a pre-programmed path, – and the human brain which is capable of *multiple* similar and new *creative* operations simultaneously. Humans can use analogy, to try to understand new concepts or problems by relating them to other situations. A computer can not.

This seems to me another reason for a more 'holographic' approach to consciousness, and consequently a more holistic approach to learning and teaching.

I find the notion of machines talking in a recognisably human way rather eerie.

Perhaps because of the human's almost automatic way of interpreting the emotional content of a sound, as much as the verbal message itself.

Since the age of 3.5 Erin enjoyed using pc educational sites. On one she liked the letters of the alphabet were displayed; and in one game a machine voice would ask her to click on a particular letter. If she got the letter wrong and encouraging voice would say, 'Try again!' If her answer was correct a delighted tone of voice would tell her, 'Well done!'

Now this is alright – not actually enjoyable but at least acceptable – because to a certain extent I can envisage the programming which would support such an apparent verbal encouragement to a learner. But it was too repetitive and automatic to be anything other than a machine game. And Erin herself never stayed playing for more than 15 or 20 minutes without deciding, 'Had enough of this Grandma.'

However, at 2.11 she had been given a doll who when her batteries were 'on' wailed with increasing volume – to me the nerve shattering cries of a bereft infant – until attended to. This meant put a bottle in her mouth and rock her.

Then her wails would turn from sobs, to hiccups, and eventually coos of delight. I was amazed at how much I disliked this programmed creature.

On the one hand I found myself unable to concentrate or think clearly if she was wailing; I was unable at some level to reject the response one would have to a real infant's cry. On the other hand I bitterly resented the effort of rocking a *doll* in order to get a bit of peace!

Similarly most adults are stressed by an infant's cry of distress and attend to it swiftly. It seems to be almost an instinctive reaction on the part of an adult to a child.

But there is one thing to be wary of here.

Yes, of course, you speak calmly and reassuringly to a young child. But, fairly early in life, certainly before the age of 12 months, children have enough experience of life to learn that though you acknowledge their needs, you do not intend to drop everything and dash to give a bottle or pick a toy off the floor or whatever.

If this sounds harsh consider a mother doing an everyday task in a kitchen with baby sitting up in his high chair observing her work.

Washing up, let's say.

Baby hollers for a drink.

Now she could stop instantly, dry her hands and get it and give it to him. But I think that once a child is at this stage of development there is no harm, and a lot of good, in holding him off verbally for a while. Remarks like, 'You want a drink. Good boy. Mummy will give it to you in a minute. You play a bit more with your toy and Mummy will soon give you your drink. Good boy.'

To delay instant gratification of demands by a continued use of a friendly helpful voice until Mother is ready, helps prevent a baby from turning into a demanding autocratic toddler. The constant praise in the above mother's speech reinforces the result she wants from baby. Patience!

A delicate balancing act is needed between responding to a cry and being later hopelessly manipulated by a pint sized tyrant!

Chapter Fourteen

Telegraphic Speech

Age 1.6–3.0

At eighteen months the 'naming explosion' is probably in full swing and the child begins to acquire new vocabulary at roughly the rate of one new word every two waking hours. He will continue to learn at this rate if not even faster right through adolescence. (Clark. Pinker.)

'Telegraphic speech' starts to appear. This refers to the short two or three word sentences common after the naming explosion. The child conveys meaning with the minimum of speech. Again these two word utterances are highly similar across cultures. All over the world children comment on things appearing, disappearing, moving about; they point out their properties and owners. They comment on people doing things, they reject and request objects and actions. They ask about who, what and where.

Here are some typical samples of two word sentences.
All wet.
No milk.
Daddy gone.
See bottle.
More hot.
Bye mummy.
My teddy.
No bread.

Telegraphic Speech

Though very brief these sentences in more than 95% of instances follow the correct word order in which they would occur in a longer more correctly structured sentence.

Here is an example of Erin using 'telegraphic speech.'

'Helen quick! Grass! Cows get up. Quick! Having a party. Yeah. A tea party. Quick Helen.'

The sample above from Erin at 1.11 shows some of the structures used. Out of context they are hard to decipher. Here is what prompted them.

We were on holiday in rural west Cork in Ireland. Erin had gone out with her parents to explore. Next door was a field with a herd of cattle who had been lying down. However being curious by nature once they spotted people by the stone wall they had wandered up to see these humans; who repaid their courtesy call by handing them really lush handfuls of grass from our side of the wall!

Erin realised that I was still in the house and missing the excitement and came dashing in to fetch me. By this stage of her life, realising that she had another grandmother apart from myself, she had moved on to calling me 'Helen'. 'Mama' had dropped by the wayside and her other grandmother was by now 'Gah mah G'enys.'

So her words on this occasion were very easy to understand, and I went out to join in the cow's tea party! Put in context the words above can now be understood quite easily.

These short sentences really open up the world for a child.

Daddy milk.

Mummy car.

Telegraphic speech works very well because of the parent's ability and willingness to interpret the child's meaning and respond to it.

At this stage children haven't dropped the repetitive babbling of the early stages, when being fed and contented, they often spend a lot of time singing and crooning 'baba' or 'dada' or similar short phrases to themselves.

The only difference now that they are older is that the repetition is of slightly different vocabulary. 'mummy see mummy see see mummy'. It seems as if the child is reinforcing his own ability to say words by constant practise of those words.

It is really quite a feat for a baby to learn to reproduce accurately all the sounds he is going to use later without much conscious effort at all. The macro effect!

Even as adults we still come across words, or groups of words we find awkward. We say, 'I can hardly get my tongue around that!' This is when momentarily how to set about saying a word has us puzzled, and we are temporarily back in the learning role of childhood.

You have to stop and think a bit before you can say tongue twisters like, 'The Leith police dismisseth us.'

A useful insight into the enormity of effort the child puts into learning.

The child will continue talking aloud for quite a few years yet. Children quite often set up a little running commentary while playing. Although as adults most of our 'talking to ourselves' is silent thought there are still occasions when we 'talk to ourselves' aloud. There is a reassurance in speaking aloud, and you may have done it yourself when say, you are reading the instructions:-

'How to assemble your new piece of furniture'.

Merely by reading you are not always 100% sure how to proceed with the task in hand. However, reading *aloud* may help. When you hear yourself *say* the next bit to do, it quite often becomes clearer what you are supposed to do.

The child needs to 'hear' himself talk, to reinforce his skill.

However, errors apart, the child is very soon stretching from two word telegraphic speech to three word fairly correct sentences, such as 'Mummy do it.' or more frequently as in Erin's case, 'No. Me do it.'

3 to 4 years

From the late Two's onward children's speech develops so rapidly that it is impossible to keep pace with their sequence of learning. The length of sentences increases steadily. They start to say more complex and correct sentences, even combining sentences, and asking involved questions.

They will still make errors, but very often this is because they encounter words which are exceptions to rules. An example of this would be a child saying,

"Mummy, I saw two sheeps."

Or

"The dog camed in the house!"

Without anyone telling them the rules of their mother tongue they are all the time deducing them for themselves. If say, book becomes books, or cup becomes cups, and so on, then logically sheep becomes sheeps!

The child is not using the one track learning style of a computer, that is to say repeating only that which he has heard.

He is acting ***creatively*** with language using knowledge gained in one setting and applying it (albeit in this instance incorrectly) to a similar situation in another setting.

He is already using analogy as a tool to aid his language skills.

Throughout his lifetime he will be learning and relearning language, refining his understanding of meaning. Each new experience he meets will require shifting language skills to cope with it.

The human brain is flexible and adaptable to changing circumstances. The computer is not. This is why human teaching is far more successful than computer teaching programmes.

This adaptability and flexibility is human ***holographic*** intelligence in action.

All that I have written so far you will have known already. Maybe some of the technical terms used by linguists might be new to you but the basic pattern you will recognise and know to be true. So that is how through hearing a child learns that sounds have meaning.

Hearing opened the world of speech, because adults provided the correct 'scaffolding'.

That is:

They gave the child a constant opportunity to hear words spoken in a way that was of interest to the child.

They used tones and pitch which he could hear and respond to.

They used speech in situations which the child was enjoying. He was playing. The richer the quality and variety of play the more language he listened to.

They didn't get upset by 'failure' or 'mistakes'. Going back to my earlier examples from Erin's speech, when she said 'bay' for 'bear' we didn't think, 'wrong!' She should say 'Bear'. We were just happy to see her communicating, and she was happy with her ability to 'get through' to us.

They also used language as a useful tool in their everyday life.

Nobody once thought too much about *teaching* the child to speak. Talking was a part of normal everyday life. They just created the right environment for speech to emerge itself.

Although I have given Erin's words above, I must admit I didn't always understand her chat as a toddler. I had to say, 'Hmm!' now and again while I hoped for some enlightenment to dawn.

No wonder people talk about the 'Terrible Twos'.

It must be tough on toddlers to have explained, clearly as far as they are aware, what it is they want or need, and then to be met with blank incomprehension. As far as possible when this happens, when the child has given a long string of earnestly spoken sounds, and is waiting for your reaction I find the only thing I can do is provide some interesting distraction.

This usually works.

Really, I think a lot of the temper and tantrums in this age group is failure to communicate. I don't like it when I know the child wants to get a message across, I am failing to understand it and we are going nowhere. I am always happier when I understand what is required. If I feel like that as an adult, then the child must feel much the same! Learning should be fun, enjoyable, with material very, very carefully selected to match the child's interests, abilities and level of vocabulary.

Chapter Fifteen

What Is It Like Being Speechless?

Being a child trying to understand and produce speech must be a little like being a tourist in a foreign land. You are in a strange country, the weather is different, the food is alien, the customs and accepted codes of behaviour and dress are unknown, the signs are in another script and you cannot understand the language.

It can be very exasperating.

Something like this happened to me in Thailand, which gave me an insight into the speechless world of the child.

I was staying at a guest house in the north of the country in a small town somewhat off the beaten track. The hotel staff spoke no English so sign language was the order of the day.

I grew frustrated by being unable to ask the price of things in the markets and shops. I had to use a guide book to get around, as I couldn't read street signs. When I came face to face with a crowd of saffron robed Buddhist monks I wasn't at all sure of the expected protocol. Do I stand aside? Do I make a donation like the locals?

Returning to my hotel I was thirsty and longing for a cup of tea. I went to the dining area and a waiter picked up an empty glass and looked at me, pointing to the glass. I knew he was offering a drink but suddenly neither water nor lemonade was good enough. I had tried earlier to get tea and been smilingly presented with a glass of thick green liquid with cream floating on top.

Quickly I did a 'thumbs up' to signal, 'Yes. I'm thirsty.'

Then I made a quick delaying gesture, one finger pointing upwards by the side of my face as I drew pencil and paper from my bag.

{This gesture is hard to describe so maybe if you do it yourself now you will 'get the message'.}

Curious the waiter drew nearer to watch what I was doing.

Discovering hitherto unexplored talents in drawing I sketched a teapot, a cup on a saucer, then on rapid reflection a round cup Japanese style, plus a jug with an arrow to a cow. By now two other staff had joined the waiter to enjoy the experience of this crazy foreigner's doings.

Carried away by my new skill, and the rapt attention of my audience I drew steam rising from the teapot. I was about to start on a sketch of women picking tea leaves from a tea bush when a burst of talk broke out and they nodded, and smiled and hurried away.

I waited experiencing tension worse than any ever envisioned by Hitchcock in his creation of thriller movies.

They returned with............

.........a pot of what I would call tea!

Total triumph!

Their pleasure was as much as mine.

One of them leant forward and carefully enunciated, 'Chai Lip Ton.'

'Chai Lip Ton.' I repeated with great satisfaction.

'Chai Lip Ton!' they all chorused.

We were a happy band, and the pleasure of that shared moment of communication lasts to the present day. Emotion obviously has a very important role in communication skills development!

They themselves expanded and developed this new knowledge. They brought tea leaves, sugar and milk and an electric kettle to my room.

Then one day, possibly needing the kettle themselves for some kitchen crisis, one knocked my door.

In his hand he held a sketch of an electric kettle! Wow! He had appropriated *my* language for himself.

I immediately fetched him the kettle whereupon he produced sketch number two.

It showed the moon, and he pointed to the sky. So it is now night time. I nodded and smiled in agreement.

It also showed the sun and he pointed to the kettle. Right. I'd get my kettle back in the morning.

Our ease of communication was immensely satisfying for all participants in the exchange.

Look at this experience and think of a child learning language.

What Is It Like Being Speechless?

Inability to communicate is very frustrating.

Discovering *how* to communicate is satisfying both for the learner and teacher. And with cooperation on both sides the doors to further advances in understanding are now possible.

Which is why I was so excited when I first heard about Baby Sign Language.

Undoubtedly without realising it many caretakers down the generations have used sign with a child to further communication. Equally the child before verbal communication has used sign, such as when a small child firmly tucks his hands under his armpits when he doesn't want to do something, like put on a coat or a cardigan; or compresses his lips and turns his head aside when he doesn't want to eat.

I hadn't noticed until reading research on Baby Sign drew my attention to it more fully, how universal sign is already, and how easy communication must be now for a parent who more *consciously* introduces sign to a child.

The real instigator of modern Baby Sign is an American doctor, Joseph Garcia. He was working with deaf parents and their hearing children. He noticed that these children who were taught Sign by their parents communicated far more, and far earlier, in this preverbal form than children without Sign.

More significantly, he noticed that invariably they also *spoke* earlier than their peers who were raised using verbal communication alone!

What a breakthrough!

He started research in this subject and refined, researched and validated his method until it was finally completed. He then launched his system to the public who immediately saw the enormous benefits of being able to communicate accurately with a preverbal infant. We now know that it takes an average of five months for a word which a child has demonstrated that he understands to appear in his own speech. If the first words on average appear around his first birthday, then it follows that sign using larger motor movements of the body, can be a means of communication from about seven months onwards!

The optimum age to start teaching is at six months. This means for me personally I am more than ever looking forward to another grandchild due shortly. I shall ensure that I and all close family members study Baby Sign and be ready for even earlier infant communication.

From reports which I have so far studied on Baby Sign I am able to say the following:

Erin's early behaviour, without us being fully aware of it at the time, showed that she would have taken to Sign like a duck to water. For instance, she rubbed her tummy for food, raised her arms to indicate up, put her hand towards her mouth like a semi-closed fist to indicate she wanted a bottle, opened and shut her hand to say 'more', and so on. Although we interpreted these signs fairly accurately, I can imagine how much better it would have been to have a definite agreement from all carers about which sign meant what.

Some early critics of Baby Sign were worried that teaching Sign would delay verbal communication from a baby. However increasing research and numerous parental reports show the opposite to be true.

I think that this is because the baby in learning Sign has learned about symbolism before learning words.

If he has grasped the idea that a *sign* can be a symbol for something else, then it is quicker and easier for him to accept that a *sound* is a symbol for something else.

This means that it is especially important for parents to speak when they sign. So if a baby signs 'up' the carer responds by verbally reinforcing the sign. 'You want up do you? Shall I pick you up then? Come on baby. Up. Up.'

Chapter Sixteen

So What Is Language?

Though I had seen before lists of the first 50 words spoken by a child it was not until I studied Erin's, and knowing the child as I did, did I see the obvious. In common with lists from other children, her vocabulary was mainly monosyllabic, single consonant utterances.
So far, fine.
Most of the words were nouns.
Fine.
Except that on reflection I saw that though her list was mainly nouns – as an English language teacher would view nouns – to Erin they were nouns or verbs *depending on how she used them!*
A preposition could be a verb.
A noun could be a verb or at the very least a command or request.
Language was not confined by any conventional rules and regulations, but was a tool to fast and accurate communication of meaning between the child and her adult minders.
It didn't matter what part of speech a word was, noun, verb, preposition, whatever. If it got the result she wanted she used it whatever way she wanted.
It was the same when I said the word for 'tea' in Thailand.
I wasn't using the word as a noun.
I was *asking* for tea.
Body language accompanying the noun was equally vital. Holding an imaginary cup to my lips, and smiling when my Thai waiter gave me

The Language Barrier

a thumbs up signal that he understood. Equally it is so with the child, stretching his limited vocabulary to almost infinite limits.

I suppose now it's about time to try to define what I mean by language.

So what is spoken language and who uses it?

I think we could agree that spoken language is made up of <u>words</u>. These words have an <u>agreed meaning</u> within a <u>community</u> using a shared language. I have underlined what we might agree are essentials to understanding one another.

For example, if you use the same language which I am using here, and if I write the word 'cup' I would expect you to get an image in your head of a one handled container used to hold fluids for drinking.

(How much easier it is to say 'cup'! Perhaps spoken language was invented by the lazy!)

We have '<u>shared meaning</u>' for a word. Our minds agree on what the word 'cup' means.

A one to one relationship exists between the object (cup) and the sound ('cup') we use to name it.

The word has become a <u>symbol</u> for the object. When I write, and you read, 'cup' we are not looking at one specific cup. We have a concept of 'cupness.' No such word as 'cupness' exists I know that; but I also know that you understand what I mean.

It is rather like ' pretend' play with children. In this kind of play anything can become something else.

For example, Erin at 2.3 had a toy phone. She pressed a button on it and got a ring tone. She answered it and called to me, 'Grandma, phone!'

I picked up a television remote control near me and held it to my ear.

'Hello!' I said. 'Is that Erin?'

Erin didn't bat an eyelid at the use of the remote but continued our pretend phone chat with enthusiasm.

Equally from about 1.6 onwards plain large cardboard boxes became cars, buses, houses, shops whatever we wanted them to be. Later at 4.11 'pretend' play was still much in evidence but had become more sophisticated. A couch would be a ship at sea in a storm, with wind and rain and a storm tossed sea. These objects, remote control, box, couch were all symbolic of what we wanted them to be, just as the spoken sound is a symbol for the words we want to say.

When Erin was 5.1 the results of some research into children's language was published by Lancaster university. According to a report of this by the B.B.C.,

So What Is Language?

'The researchers said they expected to find that children who had better cognitive development, such as being able to do a puzzle or match pictures and colours, would have better language skills.

But in fact, only the ability to pretend that one object was another object – such as pretending a wooden block is a car or hairbrush – was associated with better language skills.'

I think it is because the child who learns through 'pretend' play that one object can stand for another, finds it easier to work out that one particular sound can stand for a particular meaning.

Later they will find it easier to read because this substitution of one symbol (the printed letters of the alphabet) for another is accepted after their experience with substituting sound symbols in talk.

Now the word 'cup' names a thing existing in the outside world, which we can see and touch. The real object has an unchanging reality.

But this is not so with the *word* used to describe it.

Because if I write 'World cup' the mental image changes quite dramatically. Now the cup has two handles, not one; now it is made of metal, and not china or porcelain. It has grown significantly larger.

Also it may now release a flood of memories to your mind, football related images, and so on.

It's function too has changed. It is no longer something to drink from, but is primarily a symbol of success, an object to be held up in triumph.

I have made a similar use of language a few lines up when I wrote 'a *flood* of memories'.

This type of use of words occurs all the time: where we move in our thinking from a simple one word meaning to a more complicated idea:-

Snow man.
Market garden.
Super market.
Bat man
Flower bed.

Surprising isn't it how separate words with a fairly fixed meaning can alter so much by change of context.

So words which start life with a single meaning can effortlessly become the trigger to the brain for all kinds of complicated thoughts, emotions, memories. They lose their original simple straightforward definition. ***They activate thought.***

And if you think about it, the human brain seems to have an almost unlimited capacity to learn, accumulate, recall and use these words, both with their original definitions, and the later acquired multiple meanings.

In the example used above of World Cup neither word, cup nor world, is linked to a single object. Each has combined with the other to create a whole new train of thought and images in the mind.

These ideas which are triggered in the mind by language are called concepts.

We have started to move into the world of cognitive ability.

Words are beginning to be used not just to describe here and now reality but the world of ideas, memories, symbols, perceptions.

The means whereby the *concrete reality* of something – i.e. you can see it, touch it; it exists on earth – can be transformed into an *idea* is illustrated in an unusual way by the baskets woven by the Dogon, a tribe of West Africa. These people today are all who remain to represent what was once an ancient and sophisticated civilization.

However, remnants of their culture and highly developed levels of thinking can still be seen in some of their craft; for example, in the design of their traditional baskets.

These consist of firstly an open topped cube shaped container which represents 'the earth and material things'.

This represents something in the 'here and now', which, as I have said before, is how the infant first learns about the world around him. He believes that what he sees, feels, tastes, hears is what life is all about.

Gradually he develops a more sophisticated understanding of things. He learns for example that when he says, 'Bye bye' to someone that that someone has not disappeared out of his life forever. He begins to realise that things and people can still exist even when they are not immediately available to see or touch or hear.

This leap of understanding is represented by the Dogon in the lid of their basket which is cone shaped to symbolize the dome of the sky. The sky represents ideas and concepts, something beyond earthly reality.

Now for the final, crucial part of the basket. The lid is tied to the base by a palm frond.

The name for this palm frond is *'the word.'*

I find the simplicity of this stunning. It is such a simple design; and yet incorporates in itself an idea which has taken in the west centuries of research and study of language and human behaviour.

From the perceived reality of the child we as humans move to ideas beyond a 'here and now' reality; and the way that enables us to do this

So What Is Language?

is language. We can move beyond the 'here and now' to unlimited new thoughts and ideas!

Language has now become an essential part of our daily life. We use it in many different ways to cope effectively with our day to day existence. We use it to arrange events in lives, to maintain our friendships, to organise our personal and social engagements, and undeniably to reinforce our view of the world.

Our songs, nursery rhymes, heritage and viewpoints come through language. We rely on it to transmit our history and values and to express our hopes and fears.

Above all, language gives humans amazing intellectual power.

Unlike any other creature on this planet, we can use language to understand things outside our local world. We can go beyond a world which can be perceived by the senses alone.

We can read about and learn about the experience of others – possibly in a different time and place – and share and understand their knowledge. Animals can only perceive the 'here and now'.

Humans can go beyond that.

Language gives us this power.

Chapter Seventeen
_____

Baby Talk And Ancient Sumerian

Language allows us to share and transmit knowledge.
   Our ability to endow the human infant with speech means that each child has the chance not only to learn what his parents know, but to transmit to his own children this information, together with any further insights or knowledge discovered within his own lifetime.
   And I don't think that there is any field of study which shows this as clearly as the study of the development of spoken language itself.
   The prototype language for Europe, the Middle East, and the Indian sub continent is Sumerian. Archaeologists have evidence of spoken language – Sumerian – in Mesopotamia something like ten thousand years ago. This first spoken language developed from an earlier means of communication by facial expression, gesture and pointing.
   That is not to say that other groups of people did not in other areas develop a spoken tongue independently. For example, the click language of parts of Africa used clicking sounds to convey meaning.
   Work is still ongoing to unravel the story of the 'Family Trees' of human speech. In the meantime we do know that Sumerian is a language isolate which began and died long before many of the numerous languages spoken today. It was overtaken by Akkadian when it died out in general use in early 2,000 B.C.
   We can know the extent of Sumerian influence by the location of the spread of little baked and calibrated clay tokens or counters used for counting numbers. Each pebble or stone was a different size or shape to denote a particular number. These tokens have been found at archaeological

sites which stretch from modern day Pakistan to Khartoum in the Sudan in Africa.

There is a suggestion that these tokens may have been used to communicate numerical information *before* spoken language.

Whatever, the fact that different shapes and sizes of tokens were used to convey the idea of numbers between peoples, means that humans had understood the idea of one *object* standing for another *meaning*.

This is very similar to a child's imaginary play, where as I have already described a remote control can be a telephone. Equally, a child first learning language has to grasp the idea that certain *sounds* convey definite *meaning*.

A few points are well worth noting about the development of the Sumerian tongue.

You will quite quickly realise that this early growth of language is even today – 10,000 years down the line! – amazingly paralleled by infants today learning mother tongue.

Stage 1.

Sumerian began with what we would today call Sign Language, or if using this method with infants, Baby Sign. Gesture and body language conveyed meaning.

The contemporary infant uses facial expression and crying to signal his earliest needs.

Stage 2.

Sumerian developed into a tongue which is unique in that it used vowel sounds only to communicate meaning.

For instance 'a' meant water.

The Sumerians appear not only to have invented a complete spoken sound symbol system but more importantly to have discovered the *idea* of such a system. Other peoples who observed them communicating through sound could make a great leap forward and develop spoken language since they were now aware that it could exist!

They may or may not have taken vocabulary from the Sumerians but once they understood how the sound system worked, then invention of words for things and actions would have been simpler.

Baby goes on to develop vowel sounds before he makes sounds which we regard as 'talk'. The simplest and easiest vowel sound is 'a' and this appears first. This is followed later in babble by 'o' and 'u' (pronounced 'uh'), and 'i'.

The Language Barrier

Very early speech attempts always reveal that baby has a sounder grasp of vowel distinctions far earlier than he has a similarly confident grasp of consonants. Erin for instance never confused the vowels in her earliest 'bay' (bear), 'bah'(bath), 'Boh' (bottle) vocabulary.

Stage 3.
At this stage a consonant is joined to the vowel sound to get the first 'words'. Some early Sumerian words include:-
Na – he/she/that one (another person)
Ba – share (noun) or to give (verb)
Ma – to bind (hold close)
Da – nearness (to someone)
Pa – small canal
Baby's first words are the consonants easiest to articulate, b, d, m, n, p, followed by the 'a' vowel sound.

Stage 4
More complex words developed by combining elements of earlier meanings.
Ama – mother
Aba – lake
Dab – to hold
Ada – father
Children start to build up a more intricate lexicon of words, (like Erin's first 50 words), in order to describe needs and wants.

Stage 5
A sudden upsurge of new vocabulary which serves to differentiate better between similar, but subtly different, elements of daily life.
The child goes from the naming explosion to a time of gathering new words at a speed and rate which is formidable for any student.
This then is how archaeologists and scholars have reconstructed the stages in the beginning of spoken words by one group of the human race.
I think you will see that it is remarkable how closely the contemporary infant follows a similar pattern of development.
Now before the Sumerians had words they had *things* or objects which existed in the outside world, like water or food.
The people also performed *actions*.
So initially everyone had to agree on the speech sounds which agreed to what these things or actions were.

Baby Talk And Ancient Sumerian

Obviously this would entail gesture, and pointing. The words would all have to be in the context of the 'here and now'.

Listeners would have an aid to understanding words because the speaker could simultaneously indicate his meaning.

The first and most significant vocabulary was that used to name those vital to the survival of the infant, mother, father and related carers.

Look at the following table. It shows the words used in families to denote informally certain persons in the child's entourage.

Name of Language	Word for mother	Word for Father
Bengali	ma	baba
Apalai (Amazon)	aya	papa
Chechen	nana	da
Chinese (Mandarin)	mama	baba
Cree (Canada)	mama	papa
French	maman	papa
Greek (Modern)	mama	babbas
Icelandic	mama	pabi
Italian	mama	babso
Nahuatal (Mexico)	naan	ta
Norwegian	mamma	pappa
Quechua (Ecuador)	mama	tayta
Rumanian	mama	tata
Urdu	mah	bap
Xhosa (South Africa)	mama	tata

These languages are distant from one another by quite wide geographical areas and belong to groups of people who rarely if ever are in contact with each other. They are thousands of years in time separated from Sumerian civilization.

Yet their words for mother and father are remarkably similar.

This appears odd unless we go back to the real basics of talk. It is after all only controlling the flow of air through the mouth and nose, together with using the tongue and lips to create different sounds.

As you read through the following section, it may be that what I am saying will be easier for you to understand if you sound out the vowels and consonant combinations for yourself! The vowel sound 'a' (ah) is the most effortless. The new born's cry is a repetitive 'a' sound. Slowly however the child will start to produce the 'a' sound without actually crying – just making a noise really.

Then one fine day if the lips happen to be closed when he tries this and the 'a' has to force them open to get through the resulting sound is 'ma'. This 'm' consonant is possibly the physically easiest of all to say. If there is a listening adult this sound will be heard and the adult will interpret it as 'ma' meaning 'mother'.

Great excitement – baby is learning to talk!

From then on whenever baby produces 'ma' he will get a very positive response. So he starts to work for control of its production. In the meantime he may happen upon 'b' and 'p'. The 'b' will emerge when he pulls his lips apart while saying 'a', the 'p' if he pushes air more strongly through the lips.

So far he has needed no control of his tongue. But he has been exercising his tongue regularly by pushing it up towards his palate to suck and ensure his food supply. His tongue is familiar with this movement.

If now he is to do it while saying 'a' he will produce 'da' 'ta' or 'na', depending on which part of the palate his tongue touches.

His family pounce on this evidence of growing speech and assign meaning to his utterances.

The first appearing 'ma' indicates to family that he is naming his mother. The child will slowly learn this same meaning as he observes the results of his production of the sound. 'b', 'p' or 'd' are allocated to father, and in very many cultures the 'n' sound indicates a close carer like a grandmother, or nursemaid.

So we see 'nana', nan', 'nanny' and so on appearing in many different languages to denote another female carer.

Oddly enough, 'ni' and 'na' in Sumerian meant as you saw, 'he, she, that one,' so it was even then used as a word to refer to another human being, albeit one not so close as mother and father.

There does seem to be a very rigid 'pecking order' in the distribution of these earliest consonant and 'a' sounds, with mother being in prime position, followed by father and then other carers. The hierarchical positioning of those in the child's entourage reflects the time sequence in which the consonants first appear.

It is significant that none of these early consonant vowel words refer to younger family members. This is obviously because when baby first starts talking he cannot possibly have younger relatives! Equally his 'baba' for 'baby' can logically only refer to him himself.

To my mind what is so striking about this development of speech is how closely it follows the sequence of language development thousands of years ago by the Sumerians.

The contemporary infant in anything between twelve and eighteen months progresses through a language development that originally took many generations to perfect.

This is only possible because of the interpretation placed on his initial vocalizations by those around him.

This interpretation I would call the human **Language Endowment Device**.

Chapter Eighteen

Some Of The Elements Of Language

Within language systems we all mostly agree on the order in which we string names for objects (nouns) and action words (verbs) together so that our speech makes sense; so that it is comprehensible to a listener.

To do this we need connector words like 'the', 'a', 'and' and so on. So though we would usually say, 'I drink from a cup', we are unlikely to say, 'A cup from I drink.'

This agreement about the order of words in a sentence used within a language community is called the grammar of a language. The grammar we know can be changed to achieve special effects. Such as that used in some of the dialogue of a movie like Star Wars.

So far the word order described is as it is in English. But not all languages have the same conventions about usage.

For example, if you translate *word by word* from other languages to English, instead of translating *meaning*, you could come up with a different order of where to place items in a sentence.

So In English you might say, 'He's a strong man.'

The same sentence translated into Irish Gaelic becomes:-

Is fear láidir atá ann. Now translate this literally i.e. word for word back into English and what you get is,

'It is a strong man that is in him.' (It is man strong is in him.)

Or try Arabic.

A familiar offer of hospitality is, 'My house is your house.'

Baiti baitek.

Literal translation, 'My house your house.'

Some Of The Elements Of Language

The noun *ending* indicates who is the possessor of what. 'Bait' is a house' , the ending 'i' is mine , the ending 'ek' is yours. Or better still look at one of my favourite sentences in Arabic.
In English, 'What time is it?'
In Arabic, *'Shoof esaa-ah.'*
The literal translation is, 'See watch.'
I think this reflects much of the simplicity of a child's 'telegraphic speech'. The speaker relies on the listener to understand the implicit message, 'I would like to know the time!'

French adjective order differs from English. *Le Moulin Rouge* literally becomes The Windmill Red.

And so on in every language you can think of.

So each child has not only to learn words and what they mean but also the accepted word order for talking sensibly to others in his own speech community.

There is nothing immutable or fixed about this ordering of words to make sense, as it changes from language to language; and even *within* a language itself in the process of time. The English spoken a thousand or even five hundred years ago would be almost, if not completely unintelligible, to a modern day speaker of the same language.

The only conclusion we can then draw about grammar is that it is the order of words in a sentence, as agreed through usage, to be most likely to be understood by another speaker of the same tongue at a contemporary time in history.

Language – whether spoken, written or signed – appears to have at least four essentials:-

1. A <u>vocabulary</u> of words or symbols.
2. A <u>grammar,</u> or set of rules, about how these symbols may be used.
3. A range of <u>meanings</u> that can be communicated with these symbols.
4. A <u>community</u> of people who use and understand these symbols.

An interesting thing about grammar is that it is not fixed or immutable in any way as say is the law of gravity (or rather the *effect* of gravity whether you try to break the law or not. Joke.)

If you remember Erin's first words included a 'bay' sound for 'bear'. This was the sound she made to let us know that she wanted to watch her Bear in the Big Blue House video.

So this short sound had all the essentials of language.

The Language Barrier

'Bay' was a spoken piece of <u>vocabulary</u>, a symbol with <u>meaning</u> for family – the <u>community</u> in which she lives. In a one word sentence <u>grammar</u>, or the accepted sequence of subject verb object, does not arise!

Chapter Nineteen
___

Very Young Children Question Language

Broadly speaking, there are two ways to account for language acquisition.

The first way believes that language is learned like any other human behaviour.

The other way believes that language is innate and that no learning process is required.

Both theories do accept that language is a developmental process. There is a commonly observed progression in the acquisition, or learning, of the vocabulary and grammar of language.

The learner goes from one step in the process to the next step. For example, Erin went from one word 'sentences' to telegraphic speech, to fuller expressions of meaning. At 3.5 most basic constructions were in place apart from the odd error. These were usually with past tense of verbs, or with negation. For example:

'Did you see that Helen? I catched it myself!'

or commenting on a food new to her,

'This very not tasty!'

At 3.7 Erin had developed her own version of jokes she considered highly amusing. For example, when we picked her up from nursery school to drive her home she would ask, 'Where are we going? Are we going to school?'

As we approached a green traffic light she would announce with great hilarity, 'Look – green means stop!'

This playing with language became more sophisticated at 4.2. We had one weekend watched a television programme which included a performance by U2. Her parents in the previous month had been to a concert given by this group.

Later in the week she came to me and said, 'I really love you!' By now the adults around her had worked out that most times when she said, 'I love you' it really translated as, 'I am very happy at the moment.' However, I played along and said, 'That's good because I really love you too.'

To which she replied, 'You should say *"as well"'*. You don't want to say you love those people singing on television do you?'

She found her own wit very amusing.

Similarly her mother took her to buy a little wooden wishing well for the garden, which they had seen on a previous visit to a store, but they were temporarily out of stock. Talking about this later she told her grandad that they had been to buy a 'missing well'.

'Don't you mean a wishing well?' said her grandad.

'No. We went for a wishing well but there was none in store so it was a *missing* well!'

I think that this was the first occasion where the adults present found her joke *genuinely* amusing! But the interest in language it manifests is revealing of the thought processes at this stage of language development.

At this same time she was querying meaning of things she overheard others say.

'What does 'going to town' mean?'

'Well it means going into the city I suppose.'

'No it doesn't. Mum said she was going to town *on the garden*. She didn't say she was going anywhere!'

She was trying to understand the difference between literal and intended meaning in adult speech. Her jokes showed that she was beginning to grasp the idea of a move away from literal use of words, to using words for other purposes, in the jokes instance to amuse herself and her audience.

Studies show that bilingual children show a great awareness of how a language is used. But Erin spoke only English, in an English speaking environment. Nevertheless as a monolingual she often showed that she had the ability to think about language itself.

From about three years of age onwards Erin asked many questions about what words she had heard *meant*.

At 2.11 I was out shopping with her and a woman held a shop door for me to get the push chair through easily. I said, 'Thank you very much.'

Erin looked up at me and asked, 'What you said?'

Very Young Children Question Language

I said, 'I said "Thank you very much" to the woman because she was kind holding the door open.'

Erin was not satisfied with this. 'Why you said "very much?" she asked me.

I then realised that Erin had understood the thank you bit of the story but was wondering what was the 'very much' bit about.

As I tried to explain I felt that I probably only raised more questions in her head. I said, 'Thank you is thank you, but thank you very much is thank you, thank you, thank you!'

Fortunately she then burst out laughing and kept saying, 'Very much' most of the way home.

I had an uneasy feeling that she now believed that 'very much' was a stronger version of 'thank you', but I decided to take the coward's way out and leave well alone.

Later, at 3.4 her mother looking at some rather bedraggled hanging baskets in their back yard said, 'I'm going to be ruthless today with these baskets and empty and replant them completely.'

Erin then asked me, 'What's ruthless?'

I hesitated in replying, dismissing brutal, callous, hardhearted from my mind, trying to find a way to explain which was within her vocabulary range! Her mother saved me by simply saying, 'I'm not going to stop until all the baskets are empty!'

Another day, aged 4.3 she asked me, 'What is a diary?'

I started to reply, 'It's a kind of book, where you write things down you want to remember.'

Before I could go further, she interrupted me saying,

'It *can't* be grandma! It can't be a *book*! Mummy said she was putting the school concert in her diary!'

It seems when words don't have any sense or meaning that a child queries them.

At 5.2 she was telling me about a child who Erin claimed couldn't yet 'speak properly'. 'Do you know Grandma, she said she had eated all her food and she should have said she had eatened all her food!'

Dilemma!

What do I reply? I took the easy option and agreed with Erin. 'Oh dear. She said she had eated when she had eaten her food!'

There are numerous other examples from children showing this ability to think about words.

Shaffer in his research results quotes a child as saying, 'I be sick. Is this the right way or wrong way to say it?'

Donaldson considers this reflecting on, and questioning of, language as 'a key factor in the development of reading in young children.'

Chapter Twenty

Physical Development And Language Development Are Related

Now these steps in language growth parallel development in physical, mental and emotional growth or maturation.

I think that it is impossible to study language in isolation from the individual, and the level of cognitive, emotional and physical maturation they have reached. Much research has been done in each of these fields. – linguistic, physical, emotional and cognitive – but very often each field is studied in isolation from the others. I don't really see how this can be done effectively.

Each type of development seems to facilitate another.

Look at this outline which indicates the relationship between physical development, and language development:-

(Though the *exact* timing of each stage may differ from child to child, and his individual experiences, the *sequence* of development will be the same for all children.)

0.1 month
From birth to one month the infant has little or no controlled movement, though there is slightly improved control in head lifting when he is lying on his stomach.

He cries at loud noises and quietens when listening to gentle speech.

The Language Barrier

0.2
When lying on his stomach a baby can lift his head slightly; and his eyes are starting to follow moving objects.
As well as crying at loud noises and smiling at friendly voices he can now gurgle, grunt and sometimes say 'Ah'.

0.3
When lying on his stomach he can prop himself on his forearms, and lift up his head and chest. He can turn his head to one side when he is pulled up.
He starts making cooing sounds, recognises his parent's voices and responds to them. His parents by now can easily recognise by his vocalisations whether he needs food, company, a nappy change or is just trying out sounds for his own pleasure. In other words, he has started to use sound as a means of communication!

0.4
His head control is now greatly improved. He begins to sit alone when propped up. He sometimes accidentally rolls over from his stomach to his back.
He can now make cooing, squealing and gurgling noises, and repeat some sounds.

0.5
He can now bring his feet to his hands and mouth when he is lying on his back. He can push up on extended arms. He can roll from his back to his stomach again. He can support his own head when he is pulled from lying on his back to a sitting position.
He can laugh, coo or gurgle for attention in response to his mother's voice. He begins to respond to, 'No.'
He now not only responds to changes in tone of voice but he himself can use sounds to express emotions and wants. He pays attention to other sounds in his environment such as music or television playing, or a knock at the door.

0.6
He can easily roll from back to front, and then back again. He plays with his feet when he lies on his back. When he lies on his stomach he can shift his weight from one arm to another if he wants to reach for toys. He can now sit by himself without using his arms for support. He can pass

things from one hand to the other and uses the fingers and palm of his hand to hold unto objects.

He now starts to 'babble' and uses laughs coos and gurgles to gain attention. He responds to 'No' and uses all kinds of sounds including babbling to express his emotions.

0.7

The child now begins to pivot on his stomach and belly crawl. He sometimes pushes up on his hands and knees. He can sit independently in a high chair or similar and he can play freely with his hands as his sense of balance improves.

Very often now he can hold objects with a finger and thumb. He can use bent fingers and thumb to rake objects into the palm of his hand.

As well as utilising the language skills already acquired he now begins to imitate speech sounds like mama mama. He also responds to his own name and some other simple words like 'teddy'. As well as babbling he now uses emotion and gestures to signal what he wants.

0.8

He can easily reach for toys while sitting. He begins to rock on hands and knees and may even crawl a few steps. He can sit back on his heels to play. Some children at this age can pull themselves to a standing position primarily by using their arms though they have difficulty getting down again, and usually land back on the floor on their bottoms. When upright, some can progress some way along a couch or low table, using both hands to steady themselves.

He now responds to his name and listens when spoken to. He can imitate sounds and recite syllables like 'ba' 'ma' or 'da'. He smiles to show that he is pleased and loves noisy toys, like rattles. He uses body language to signal his wishes – for instance at mealtimes, closed lips and head turned away means, – 'Don't try to feed me more. I've had enough!'

0.9

The child can now use a variety of leg positions when he is sitting. He can move from sitting to a hand and knees position. When in a standing position using a couch or table for support, he can move, his body partly facing the way he is going, using his hands to help maintain his balance. He can crawl around quite easily. He is able to grasp small objects between his thumb and index fingertip.

The Language Barrier

Apart from responding to his name he starts to show that he recognises the names of others in his environment. He responds to simple words like 'bottle', 'walk', 'bath', and so on. He imitates a variety of the sounds he hears around him. He may wave 'Bye bye' or raise his arms for 'up'.

0.10
When he is sitting he can reach in all directions. He can kneel on one knee, and from this position can pull himself to standing. He can also now lower himself to a sitting position without thumping his bottom unto the floor. He can walk using only one hand to balance on a piece of furniture. His wrist is now extended when he wants to grasp something.

He can now call or shout for attention. He responds to simple commands such as, 'Come here.' He babbles a lot; most of it unintelligible to a listener though parts are clear like 'mama' or 'baba'. He laughs, and may imitate sounds like a cough. He shows that he enjoys music, and the rhythm of nursery rhymes, especially ones which involve physical involvement like 'Pat a cake' or 'Round and round the garden.'

0.11
He is now able to squat and return to standing while holding on to some support. He can play in a kneeling position and sit with his legs straight out in front of him. He can hold objects between his thumb and first two fingers. He can stand, but not walk, alone. He can shift his weight from one foot to the other if his hands are held.

He engages in 'conversation' with his carers, i.e. his babble 'turn takes' when he is being spoken to by others. He can point out the answers when asked some 'where' style questions; 'Where is teddy? Where is daddy?' Etc. He responds to requests correctly such as ,'Give me the ball'.

0.12
He may now try to walk alone. There is no arm swing when walking, and frequent loss of control with bumpy sit downs on the floor. He cannot carry anything when walking. It requires his total concentration. His gait may be very stiff, he swings his legs from the hip.

He may produce his first recognisable words, most likely 'mama' or 'dada.' He begins to babble sounds like sentences, though his listeners do not recognise actual words he <u>sounds</u> as if he is engaging in conversation. He enjoys music and bounces in his seat or jigs on the spot with a *supporting piece of furniture. He can nod or shake his head in quite clear meaning of 'Yes' and 'No'.*

The progressive parallel development of language and motor skills here is clear enough for anyone to see.

Once he gains more control of standing and walking the first real words appear. After this the 'naming explosion' begins. At the same time as this rapid increase in vocabulary, there is an equally dramatic improvement in motor skills.

He can walk quite easily and soon begins to jump, run, dance and so on. Of course there are many falls and knocks but nothing seems to daunt his enthusiasm. He may have difficulty staying upright or changing direction when he moves; but he struggles to overcome this; and *the more physical control he gains so also his language skills expand.*

And as language is only the external evidence of inward thought so his cognitive abilities are also developing.

And all of this is because the child wishes to be independent, to control his environment. He wants to walk and play and talk. Children show this quite clearly as soon as they are able to say, 'No. Me do it!'

Once children can use the basics of communication in speech it is not so easy to see their progress as clearly as before.

However, Halliday describes a developmental sequence of the functions of speech used by children; this can be useful when trying to provide a child with a linguistically rich environment.

1. Talk used to communicate the child's preferences, wants or needs.

Give me...
I want...

2. Talk used to express his individuality.

Here I am.
Watch me...

3. Talk used to interact with others; to plan, develop or maintain a game or play activity.

You and me can be.....
I'll be the Mummy......

4. Talk used to control, make rules, or to give instructions.

The Language Barrier

Do as I tell you...
You need to ....

5. Talk used to explain.

I'll tell you.....
I know...

6. Talk used to find things out, to wonder, to hypothesize.

Why did you do that?
Why do....
What for?

7. Talk used to create, explore or entertain.

Let's pretend...
I'll tell you a story....

Making provision for the possible use of *every* kind of talk helps to develop the child's speech and intelligence to the maximum.

Chapter Twenty One

The Role Of 'Emotional Response' In Speech

What is often ignored – perhaps because people are not too sure about mixing the emotional and cognitive functions in the human mind – is the emotive or affective aspect of learning.

Whereas I really believe that for learning to be effective it must be affective.

Suppose you ask a child why he goes to school. The choice of answers usually boils down to one of two options: try it on a child yourself and see. The options are:-

I go to school because I have to.
I go to school because I want to.

Which response would you prefer to hear?
Which child do you think finds learning easier?

And while we're on this subject sometimes a child starts to refuse school, or show that they are unhappy when as far as we know there is no clear reason for this behaviour. This is where I think it important that *before* a child starts school they learn how to express feelings. No one can tell you why they are worried if they haven't got the words to express the cause of the worry.

It is quite easy to teach this type of vocabulary.

The Language Barrier

For example, Erin had walked the length of a foot high wall in her garden. She was very proud of her achievement and asked me to have a go at doing the same.

I went for an Oscar, and looked very doubtful. 'I feel nervous! I might fall and hurt myself! That wall makes me feel nervous!'

She coaxed me to have a go, assuring me that she would hold my hand. I got up, and wobbled dramatically. 'Oh! I'm still nervous!'

'You're all right grandma! You won't fall; don't be nervous.'

Great.

She had said the word herself and understood it.

In a similar fashion you can cover the vocabulary and understanding of most of the emotive language of a child, happy, sad, bored, worried whatever you think is needed for good communication.

Now the reason that I put this here is that Erin came out from nursery one day almost incoherent with the need to tell us of her adventures that day. She had come out from school obviously stressed. Fortunately at 3.8 she had the vocabulary to explain why. She had been with a teacher and other pupils to a country park. As they pulled up the teacher noticed at a distance back that there was the bloodied body of a squashed squirrel in the road. She had the children line up and follow her back to the corpse. Here she explained that the animal had been run over and was now dead. They could know this by observing the blood around its mouth.

Erin's mother rang the teacher to confirm the accuracy or otherwise of this bit of teaching. The teacher said, 'Oh yes! Part of nature studies and the cycle of life and death.'

We were not happy with this.

Perhaps you would think otherwise.

Whatever; help your child be prepared for what they may encounter outside the home. Teach them the language they need to express their feelings.

If emotion in your opinion sounds too frivolous to mention with regard to learning perhaps I should expand a little on research and studies in this field.

Emotion is defined as any strong feeling such as joy, sorrow or fear. The word itself comes from a Latin word 'movere' meaning 'to move'. You will notice that the modern word emotion still contains the root meaning of motion. It is to 'move' a person in some way. I would suggest that it is to move their thinking in a new way.

The Role Of 'Emotional Response' In Speech

Researchers often refer to emotion as 'affect'. Perhaps because the underlying emotion 'affects' the way we behave or react to events occurring in our day to day life.

Now it is common to dismiss an argument or speech as 'emotional' rather than 'rational'. It is implied that emotion somehow invalidates the truth of what the speaker has said.

But it is the wish or desire, or the wanting, to achieve a particular effect in the listener, that the speaker has chosen which words to use in the first place. What he wishes to say may be extremely rational, and his choice of words is therefore logical in that it produces the end result which he desires.

But his original wish to speak *has* to be emotional in origin. He feels that these words *must* be spoken. He knows as a gifted speaker that he must *first* appeal to emotion in order to activate a rational response from his listeners. He knows that their response can only be based on an initial 'moving' of their mind to the facts of his case. He must 'affect' them with his choice of wording.

Take:

I have a dream.

or

Think not what your country can do for you, but what you can do for your country.

Or

We will fight them in the ditches.

All these are highly emotive statements but designed with very logical purposes.

All of these are quotes from very public statements. And all are on the surface of it very emotional. But all have had a very definite effect on the behaviour and attitudes of millions of people. They have achieved their logical, reasoned, rational aims by appealing to the emotions; which in turn have triggered the implementing of very rational goals in society, which ultimately benefited all.

I would strongly suggest that emotion comes before cognition in all use of language.

But in general western cultural assessment, emotion is regarded as personal and confined to the home and domestic situations. This viewpoint probably developed with the restructuring of our society from family run enterprises, like subsistence farming, or craft work, to the contemporary norm of working outside the home.

Outside the home, on the face of it at least, decisions must be rationalised. If, say, you want to ask a boss in a business or organisation where you work for a rise, you propose rational reasons why this should be paid to you. You do not say, 'My wife is making my life hell for me because we are always short of money for the treats she wants in life. Please, give me a rise and make both of our lives happier!'

But it is this type of emotion which is behind your apparently reasoned request for more money 'in view of your additional responsibilities' or 'to keep pace with inflation'; or whatever else your intelligence can come up with to support your need to implement your emotional wishes.

For Vygotsky the emotional aspect of learning was central. Although implicit in his earlier writings on the Zone of Proximal Development he only makes this really clear in one of the two documents on which he was working concurrently at the time of his very early death at the age of 37.

Since western education systems today have wholeheartedly endorsed his earlier work they have, as far as I can see, paid scant attention to this later work. Maybe this is because it was not available in English until 1999, and was largely unknown outside of Russia; and also, as I have said earlier, the tendency of modern culture to dismiss as irrational and invalid theories which give credence to the value of emotion in human judgements.

It is true that The Foundation Stage of the National Curriculum in England mentions 'Social, Emotional and Personal Development' as one of its required elements in the nursery curriculum. However this is only very slowly being implemented; though where it has been done properly the nurseries have become outstandingly successful. What a pity it is not equally carried forward to further up the school system!

Vygotsky wrote that thought 'is not born of other thoughts'. On the contrary he believed that thought had its origins in 'our inclinations and needs, our interests and impulses, and our affect and emotions'.

So Vygotsky's zone of proximal development, which has been demonstrated to be an ideal learning environment in innumerable homes and classrooms, has integral to it a place for affect, or emotion.

Think about it yourself. The most obvious learning situation for most people is the classrooms they attended as children. We tend to ignore the multiplicity of skills and knowledge we acquire *outside* of school or university – because we *wanted* to know. On reflection you will realise that most of what you know is learned outside a classroom.

Still early years have a strong hold on us.

The Role Of 'Emotional Response' In Speech

Which subjects did you find easy at school?
Which difficult?
Which teachers did you value?
Which of them did you dread?
Can you see any connections here?

A report from UNICEF in 2007 on the state of the world's children found that in the U.K. – the fourth richest economy in the world – fewer children in Britain 'like school a lot' (81%) than elsewhere.

Do you think that perhaps emotion comes into the equation somewhere along the line?

Would you think it would be harder or easier to learn a new topic with a caring teacher who genuinely wanted you to know as much as themselves, praised your efforts and smoothed the way to understanding; or would you prefer the one who knew it all, and was appalled at your failure to grasp facts which to the teacher were almost self evident?

All of us to some extent or another have had personal experience of both types of teacher.

Some researchers in different fields have reached somewhat similar conclusions as far as the role of emotion in cognition are concerned.

Wells, (1999) for example, concludes that 'Learning in the ZPD involves all aspects of the learner – acting, thinking and feeling.'

Brothers, (1997) sees emotion as interactive, something which is shaped by every human social communication exchange.

Other research like that of Damasio (1999) has shown emotion to be linked to specific brain structures, and that the way it is expressed is determined by social interaction. Damasio shows emotion and reason to have mutually reinforcing roles in human behaviour.

He explored the physiological relationship between emotion and cognition. He discovered that with *emotion as a trigger the brain releases what he calls 'chemical messages' which have a major impact on the efficiency of cognition skills.*

Schumann (1990) explained the significance of a gland in the brain called the amygdala. Its function is to evaluate incoming emotional data and then relay *'chemical messages'* to other centres of emotion in the brain. Once these centres are alerted by the incoming messages they *can influence what is actually perceived and learned by an individual.*

This research all seems to confirm what is obvious really: that human beings learn throughout their lives, *through their social relationships.*

And social relationships, to one extent or another, involve an emotional response.

As Benjamin Disraeli puts it, 'Never apologize for showing feeling. When you do so, you apologize for the truth'.

A supportive adult gives a child the confidence to achieve competence in a skill or task. Another style of teacher, who sees knowledge as power, and in no way intends to share this power, inhibits confidence and learning.

Chapter Twenty Two

Theories of Language: Skinner

There are quite a number of theories to explain how a child learns to speak.

Some of them appear to contradict one another; but very often these contradictions disappear when you look more closely at what each theorist is saying. I think that each holds some of the clues needed to completely understand how a child reaches proficiency in language use.

It's rather like the ancient Indian fable telling the story of some men and an elephant. They were all blind but wished to know what an elephant was really like. So they went together to visit one. There are many versions of the story but the essence of the parable is always the same. This account here is based on a fairly recent – (by the American, John Godfrey Saxe 1817–1887) – version of the parable.

The first man felt the side of the elephant and jumped back saying, 'He is like a wall!' The second man found first the elephant's tusk, and felt that it was smooth, long and sharply pointed. 'An elephant is like a spear!' was his conclusion. The third man came in contact first with the trunk – and decided that the elephant was a type of snake.

I'm sure you can already see where this story is heading! Very likely you have met with it before now.

The fourth man felt the elephant's leg. 'The elephant is strong and sturdy like a tree!' was his conclusion. The fifth decided however that the elephant was like a large fan as the part he felt was the ear. The sixth man caught the elephant by the tail and decided that an elephant was just like a rope.

Now in a modern version of the fable put to verse, John Godfrey Saxe draws the moral that each – though partly right – was in the wrong.

I would suggest a slightly different, and I believe, equally valid, conclusion. All were right in so far as their research into the animal's appearance was concerned. Each added a further and valuable contribution to an overall picture of the animal. From the perspective of each, the conclusion each drew was legitimate.

If they had shared their perspectives, instead of arguing, – and arguing is what every version of the tale has them doing – then they would inevitably have come to a more complete understanding of the truth.

In the same manner, each carefully argued theory of language acquisition brings us nearer to a real understanding of the processes involved.

Since there *are* so many theories, one initial conclusion *must* be that these processes are extremely complicated and extraordinarily complex.

If we want to help children learn then pretty obviously it is useful to know *what processes they use* to learn.

Take a look at some of the most famous researchers and their conclusions.

1 Language is learned like any other form of human behaviour. (Skinner)

2 Humans are born with an 'innate capacity' to learn language. (Chomsky)

3. Children deduce the meaning of social situations, and then work out the language needed to express this meaning. (Mcnamara)

4. Cognitive development comes before language development. (Piaget)

5. Language needs social 'scaffolding' to develop. (Bruner)

6. Language is biological and species specific. (Lennenberg, Chomsky)

7. Language is the result of social interaction. (Vygotsky, Jerome)

That language is learned like any other form of human behaviour is the theory put forward by B.F. Skinner, author of 'Verbal Behaviour' published in 1957. Skinner also says that parents teach language by offering correct models of usage for the child to imitate and by correcting their children's mistakes.

He believed that speech was quite simply a 'learned behaviour'. It depended on an individual's environment, and his personal sensory history (the knowledge he has gained through his five senses). The experiences he had had in life would shape the language he would speak. He saw language as a result of the child's interaction with his environment and his unique personal history.

His argument was that children learn language by copying or imitating adults. They learn meaning and grammar when adults reinforce what the child says, or extend it, to demonstrate a grammatically correct utterance.

So for example, a child says, 'Ball!' and her parents hand her a ball. They acknowledge that the word has meaning. They reinforce her 'verbal behaviour' by a reward response. A correct use of language is reinforced by approval, and consequently a good feeling in the child, who will then wish to gain this good feeling again. And so learn speech.

They might also say, 'Did you want a ball? Here is your ball,' to encourage further grammar and vocabulary 'behaviour'.

A speaker of English then has learned a *set of verbal behaviour* to allow him to respond appropriately to conversations in the English language. He goes so far as to say that a speaker of say, English, doesn't have a knowledge of the *language* as such so much as a knowledge of a 'set of behaviours' which allow him to function appropriately in conversations conducted in that language.

Skinner must be at least partly correct in that children speak the language of their parents, with similar grammar, structures, accents and intonation.

Chapter Twenty Three

Children Have A Language Acquisition Device: Chomsky

This theory of imitating verbal behaviour differs radically from the theory of linguist Noam Chomsky. He argued that humans are born with 'an innate capacity' to learn language.

He called this innate capacity a Language Acquisition Device, or LAD for short.

He composed a completely meaningless sentence to prove some of his points.

This sentence was, 'Colourless green ideas sleep furiously.'

Chomsky used this sentence to demonstrate some reasons why Skinner's conclusions were inaccurate.

First, a sentence can be grammatical correct, yet at the same time, be completely meaningless. Chomsky pointed this out as evidence that humans don't learn grammar based on what words actually mean.

Besides, even for a sentence which we have never heard before, we can say whether it is grammatically correct or not. Our conclusion is not based on having heard that specific sentence before. It is not something we have been taught, and learned.

His final conclusion is superb in its genius and simplicity. Humans do not learn language by mere imitation because we can produce, and understand from others, absolutely new sentences which we have never heard before.

I agree that this demonstration is very thought provoking.

CHILDREN HAVE A LANGUAGE ACQUISITION DEVICE: CHOMSKY

However.

If you *intend* a sentence to be meaningless then by all means invent such a one; and you will find it relatively easy to do so. But a prime function of words is to convey a meaning to some listener. That is what most people use language for – to convey meaning for one purpose or another. You may think that I'm missing the whole point of Chomsky's argument here.

I don't think that I am.

The whole structure of the sentence is what we would call grammatical because it follows the pattern we have used unconsciously all our speaking lives. Remember what I said about a 'human macro'? The brain *almost automatically* decodes according to the formula which has previously allowed us to access meaning. When however the message is *still* hidden it takes only split seconds for the listener to realise that the sentence is very cleverly constructed to *be* meaningless. Chomsky's whole argument hangs on us seeing just how meaningless it is.

And so in a mental double take we understand his deeper intent, rather than his surface meaning!

His second conclusion is, again on the surface, true. But all of the *individual words* in the sentence have been met before and understood in their original meanings. We have, again unconsciously, learned where to place each item to convey sense.

Should this order be reversed we can quite quickly decode it; if the sentence itself was originally *designed* to make sense. An example of this from Star Wars which caused no difficulty to cinema audiences worldwide. Everyone could decipher Yoda's meaning in such sentences as:

'Many truths we cling to, greatly to our own point of view they depend.'

Indeed very rapidly we adjust to this order and almost expect it. So there is no problem with others like:-

'There is no why. Clear your mind of questions. Then understand you will'.

'Try not. Do. Or do not. There is no try.'

But again it seems to me that Chomsky *did not want the sentence to make sense* if he were to prove his point about unconscious word order acquisition.

I think that his insights show real genius, and his manner of explaining was perhaps the *only possible way to* explain.

His third conclusion – (that we can understand brand new sentences that no one has ever said before) – is remarkable for drawing attention to the extraordinary creativity of human beings with language.

A child in telegraphic speech may say, 'Mummy sock.' It is very unlikely that he has heard this sentence spoken before!

But it does not completely demolish the Skinnerian perception of language learnt by imitation and positive reinforcement. This is because initially each item in the sentence must have been acquired in just such a manner.

Apart from which, by the time a child is producing his first words he has learned the *idea* of language, in the sense that he knows at least that sounds provoke some sort of a reaction.

When he says things like 'Mummy sock' he definitely is not copying a sentence he has heard before; but equally he is using vocabulary he *has* heard before. He knows that the sound 'mummy' *means* Mummy and 'sock' *means* sock.

And most important of all is the fact that when a child speaks, what he says *always makes sense to himself.* His utterances are internally coherent. *He* knows what he means.

For the listener it's a different kettle of fish! Does 'Mummy sock' mean:

Mummy this is my sock.
Mummy where is my sock?
This is mummy's sock.
Put on my sock mummy.

The only way to identify what the very small child means by 'mummy sock' is contextual clues, body language and intonation. *Somebody* must interpret the child's utterance.

Chapter Twenty Four

How Does It Feel To Be A Speechless Child?

The 'mummy sock' style of speech I have just described, vividly reminds me of my own painful attempts to communicate in countries – Kuwait, Pakistan, Thailand – where I spoke a *very* minimalist vocabulary. When having uttered one or two key words in the second language such as, 'Bus station where?', I would regard my listener intently to see whether or not my intended meaning had got through. I imagine the early speaking child is not much different; except in so far as he usually expects the adult to decipher quite easily, and is capable of getting very annoyed if they don't!

Speaking of grammar, I never gave it a second thought. It was bad enough learning key nouns – which could be used as verbs by altering body language and tone of voice – without fussing about grammar.

For example, *'kitab'* means 'book' in Urdu. I could get a book by saying *'kitab'* and looking round enquiringly. One day the person I asked called to some others,

'Helen ki kitab kaha hai?'

Pretty obviously I recognised my own name and also *'kitab'* a book. Hah! So *kaha hai* must be the magic formula for, 'Where is it'?

Anything I wanted from then on from a shop, to a park, to a drink or whatever it was and knew the name of, I attached the words *'kaha hai'* and got a much better response than previously.

It was ages before I realised that *kaha hai* was two separate words, and even though I had been using *hai* in simple sentences like, *'Dhobi hai'*

103

– (the laundryman is here – literally 'laundryman is') – I did not connect the two.

When I did I was amazed.

Because I suddenly realised that had I been formally taught the word order in Urdu sentences it would have slowed up my speech considerably because I would have had to think about in what order to put words, as well as recalling the words to express my meaning.

'Helen of book where is?'

'Laundryman is.'

Seemed to me quite difficult compared to my unthinking tagging sentences without at all realising that the grammar structure was very different to that of English, or indeed of what *exactly* word for word I was saying, except that *it worked*. So grammar slipped in with the vocabulary.

And indeed Skinner's notion of language as 'verbal behaviour' seemed to me to be validated by my own experiences. I used a string of sounds to achieve my aim; I copied the verbal behaviour of others to achieve the response I wanted.

No one can ask a child how they learn to speak their first language; but maybe if we observe ourselves learning another language *in a similar setting* we may get some idea of what happens. By a similar setting I mean that we have no interpreter there to help us, and that we must rely purely on ourselves and our understanding of talk around us. This 'understanding of talk' implies an ability to read a situation and draw conclusions from what we see and hear.

Children deduce the meaning of social situations, and then work out the language needed to express this meaning. (Macnamara)

John Macnamara, has made an intensive study of language acquisition, and he holds that children, rather than having an in-built language device, have an innate capacity to read meaning into social situations. It is this capacity that makes them capable of understanding language, and therefore learning it with ease, rather than a LAD.

The child first works towards understanding *'what happens'* when particular sounds are spoken. Infants learn their mother tongue by first working out *independent of language* the meaning of a situation; and thus the *meaning* a speaker intends to convey by the sounds he makes. The infant then goes on to work out the relationship between the meaning and *the verbal expression* of it they heard.

This was the method I found myself using when acquiring rudiments of other languages. And undoubtedly Skinner's 'imitation' of other's speech or 'verbal behaviour' played a key role when it came to expressing meaning.

Of course I also had the co operation of those around me. While Chomsky describes eloquently his Language Acquisition Device, and examines carefully what happens in the learner, he doesn't seem to pay as much heed to the people around the child.

Yes. I was able to 'deduce rules' from the language I heard around me.

According to Chomsky's theory I *could* learn because my brain is equipped with a 'Language Acquisition Device'.

But I could never have done this *without* the people around me.

This is why I believe that, running parallel with Chomsky's Language Acquisition Device, human beings – once they start to talk themselves – have an equally effective Language Endowment Device. This could be abbreviated to L.E.D.

So, in a sense, Chomsky's L.A.D. must be L.E.D. to speech! To a certain extent this aspect of language learning has already been examined by Bruner whose ideas I shall describe in the next chapter.

Chapter Twenty Five

Bruner's LASS

The social aspect of language has been explored and described by Bruner. He puts forward the idea of a Language Acquisition Support System (LASS). Bruner claims that it is a LASS that makes it possible for a child to learn to talk. It is a *system* which helps the infant to master a variety of uses of language.

This system depends on a particular type of social interaction which normally takes place in human development.

According to Bruner, this type of special social interaction – which I will describe in a moment – provides the preparatory work needed to get speech possible in a child. It is also the system which ensures that language learning proceeds in the correct order, and at the pace which it normally does with most children.

This special social relationship has the following hallmarks:

It must be conducted in a manner which uses language in *two way interactive* speech where speaker and listener *share the same anticipated outcome*. They are both interested in what the other has to say, and keen to understand one another.

This is as simple as a mother saying, 'Do you want to come to mama then?' and holding her arms out to an infant. She waits for a 'reply'. The reply can be as simple as the child lifting his own arms to be lifted up. 'Mama' reacts by picking up the child who responds with smiles or gurgles of appreciation. A two way, interactive, and emotion charged 'conversation' has taken place.

In a slightly older child it can be more complex.

'Would you like us to make a cake for Daddy's tea? We've got all the things we need here to make one.'

The child, whom we will take here to be four or five years old, understands the words used in the sentence: they are words relating to here and now.

Take 'Would you like to make Daddy a cake for tea?' She knows that 'you' in the talk is she, the child, herself. She knows who 'Daddy' is. She knows what a 'cake' is and as she has seen her mother baking she understands how you can 'make' a cake.

Here again, apart from Bruner's LASS there is evidence of Skinner's notion of language as *behaviour*. Mother's suggestion guides the child to an activity that mother approves of. The result should be a busy happy child and a pleased father. Mother uses language to create a situation she wants; to influence behaviour.

The language used has another quality. It *presupposes shared knowledge*. This sentence uses language which the speaker believes the listener to understand – both the words which make up the sentence itself and, more importantly, its implications. She knows that 'tea' is the family evening meal. The child knows the significance of a cake at tea. It is something which makes an occasion more special.

Daddy has often shown that he is very proud of his daughter and her skills. If *she* makes the cake, and not mother, he will be impressed. Mother will help her all the way because after all it is mother's suggestion. The child supposes like mother that 'daddy' – a specific person she knows – will be pleased.

Bruner calls this sort of social interaction a *'format'*.

A format could be described as a scenario. Within this format the child's speech develops because he is part of a conversation which involves himself. His learning is helped by the fact that he wants to find his own feet in the world and socially interact with others.

His wish to do this encourages his will to learn. So it is *emotion* (his wish) *which drives his intellect* (his will).

Certain factors are important in a format:

1. Children have a need for quality time with their parents or caretakers. This is a time when the child is the centre of attention.

2. Parents modify their speech to motherese or child directed speech when talking to children.

This adoption of simple, repeated words and phrases, spoken in a higher pitch, and using a cooing pattern of inflection, seems to be an inbuilt characteristic of any human old enough to recognise that they are speaking to a very young child. Certainly, no matter what their mother tongue, it is universally used speaking to infant learners worldwide.

Oddly enough it is much the same tone of voice as that used by pet owners talking to their pets! Here again the speaker recognises that the listener – the pet – needs help to understand what is being said.

When Erin arrived as an infant we had a dog called Luther. It soon became obvious that Luther, used to the tone of voice we used talking to him, was confused when we spoke to Erin. Say Erin had just woken from sleep and her mother, Sarah, was greeting her, – 'Hello, Erin? Are you waking up? Is my little baby waking up?' – poor Luther would hear the sound of her voice and come to where she was in the house. He would then sit and watch carefully, looking at Sarah, as if wondering why has she called me?

He persisted in appearing thus for quite a few weeks before it slowly dawned on him that Erin apparently must be just another puppy in the household. He then started to ignore motherese overheard around the house, unless it was clearly directed to him himself.

Equally if an adult non English speaker wants information from you, you must then adapt your speech to accommodate what you believe to be his comprehension level.

3. Parents and carers scaffold, or support, communication by providing regularly repeated routines. In these routines familiar phrases are consistently used.

These are routines like getting up in the morning, getting ready for going out, mealtimes, going to bed at night.

'Have you got your pyjamas?' 'Have you cleaned your teeth? Let me see your lovely teeth.' And so on.

4. Children are treated by their caretakers as proper partners in a two way process of communication. Carers speak to the infant as if he understands every word they say.

5. One special property of formats involving an infant and an adult, is that there is an imbalance between the partner's abilities. The adult knows what things are about, the child either doesn't know at all, or knows less.

6. Using environmental clues inherent in the routine children are able to work out for themselves the messages in any words spoken.

7. The language forms are learned as a result of practical usage. They are most frequently the language needed to name or ask for things.

8. Eventually the child 'takes over' the language of the routine for himself. As Bruner writes, 'The adult serves as model, scaffold, and monitor until the child can take over on his own.'

It is within such clearly defined and emotionally secure routines that the child first absorbs the ways in which language is used. The things that carers say become part of the format. They accompany the activity in easily understood and predictable ways. Gradually, the child moves from a passive position to an active one, from being an observer to being a participant. Eventually he takes over the actions of the caretaker, and, finally, the caretaker's language as well.

It is this *two way* and *affective* nature of the setting for language which Chomsky seems to ignore in his L.A.D.

Chapter Twenty Six

More Skilled Speakers Help Less Skilled

It is said that Chomsky's 'Language Acquisition Device' needs a 'Language Acquisition Support System' to operate effectively. That is to say, every L.A.D. needs his L.A.S.S.!

But I think that language acquisition goes beyond either of these. Because it seems so inborn, so instinctive in human beings to adapt their language to a less fluent speaker, we tend not to notice the process.

But once you start to consider this phenomenon it becomes more and more obvious that – whether or not infants have a L.A.D. – older, more competent speakers definitely have an ability to <u>endow</u> language.

Humans have an amazing ability to interpret another's stage of progress in a language, and adapt their speech accordingly.

And they have this even at a very young age.

I once saw a four year old scolding a seven year old who was talking to a toddler younger than either of them. The older child was annoyed with the toddler, and to aggravate her in return she had just spoken to her in a very adult fashion. The four year old was very indignant, and flew to the toddler's defence.

'Don't speak like that! You know she can't understand you! Don't be so mean!'

So, as early as four, the child fully understood the need to adapt tone and vocabulary when speaking to a toddler.

Animals are very restricted in the sounds they can make.

People talk about their pets 'understanding' what they say and I know with Luther a dog we had until recently – he died in September – we were quite unconsciously interpreting his barks, growls and other canine noises!

If this sounds ridiculous it is not.

Perhaps because I am very interested in communication in any form I became interested in how much a dog, a family pet can *really* understand. That is to say, when someone says, 'My dog understands every word I say!' this is very much an exaggeration. They can't and they don't understand *every* word said.

However I knew that Luther had *some* comprehension skills, so I decided to count how many words he definitely understood. The grand total was thirty four and included words like walk, sit, down, stay, lead, ball, bed, in, out and so on. His behaviour showed that he also knew the names of everyone in the family.

He could recognise the individual engine noise of a car belonging to family. He would get up to greet the driver long before there was a note in the distant engine to indicate that the car would stop. He ignored other traffic.

But while I was engaged in observing this I noticed something which for me was even more interesting. Everyone in the family, without being consciously aware of it, was interpreting Luther's different barks with incredible ease.

For example, one day we heard from the living room Luther barking in the kitchen. My daughter said to her husband, 'Listen. The dog needs to go out for a wee. Would you open the back door for him?'

As he rose to do this I suddenly realised that we did this type of thing all the time. Got exactly what it was the dog was *saying*!

I was very excited but didn't mention what I was thinking for a week or two. I wanted everyone to continue behaving as usual without altering any aspect of their normal behaviour with the dog.

By the end of a week I had heard enough.

'Could someone answer the door. Luther is saying someone is there.'
'Could someone take Luther in the garden for a bit? He wants to play.'
'Luther wants his breakfast.' etc.

These observations and many more like it were made when the dog was out of sight and the speaker used only the sound of his bark to interpret his needs. When I pointed this out at last everyone agreed with me, and were quite amazed to realise what had been going on!

So while it may be true that humans have a Language Acquisition Device, equally they have what could be termed a corresponding and parallel 'Endowment of Meaning Device'!

Here you may recall the earlier analysis of infant and Sumerian languages. Once the Sumerians had *agreed on a meaning* for a word, (eg. Ama is the older female who looks after you) then the word first spoken by the infant would be *endowed* with this meaning.

Chomsky, quite rightly, is very probably, the best known and most influential linguist of the twentieth century. He certainly revolutionised thinking about language and provoked numerous, (occasionally quite heated!) debates.

He doesn't write about 'learning' language; rather he writes about the child 'acquiring' language. In other words most first language is learned so apparently effortlessly that the learner is unaware of the process taking place at all.

Now, in school learning, most of us are only too aware of the amount of effort involved. So it would be invaluable to understand this acquisition process; and then, deliberately, in classrooms, recreate the conditions it needs to happen .

If this is possible – and I see no reason why not – then children at all stages of education could learn effortlessly and enjoyably.

Now, many people find the idea of a so called 'language acquisition device' as a bit of verbal sleight of hand. To say that you learn to speak because you have *an inbuilt capacity to learn to speak* does not seem like an explanation of what happens in a child's mind as they develop language skills.

However if you consider carefully what Chomsky says his whole concept becomes clearer.

To begin with he claims that we are born with a set of rules about language in our heads which he refers to as the 'Universal Grammar'. The universal grammar he explains is the basis upon which all human languages build. Chomsky gives a number of reasons why this should be so.

Among the most important of these reasons is the ease with which children acquire their mother tongue. He claims that it would be little short of a miracle if children learnt their language in the same way that they learn mathematics or how to ride a bicycle.

This, he says, is because:

"Children are exposed to little correctly formed language. When people speak, they constantly interrupt themselves, change their minds, make slips of the tongue and so on. Yet children manage to learn language all the same.

Children do not simply copy the language that they hear around them. They deduce rules from it, which they can then use to produce sentences that they have never heard before."

Because the child's knowledge of language is so complex, and learned in such a very short time, he concludes that this "internalised knowledge must be limited very narrowly by some biological property."

Children are born, then, with the Universal Grammar 'wired' into their brains. This grammar offers a certain limited number of possibilities – for example, over the word order of a typical sentence; as word order is standard in their mother tongue.

This word order is not the same in all languages. But it seems that when the child begins to listen to his parents, he unconsciously recognises which kind of a language he is dealing with – and he will set his grammar to the correct word order for his own language. Chomsky called this *'setting the parameters'*.

It is almost as if the child were offered at birth a certain number of hypotheses, or theories of grammar. He then matches his theory of grammar with what he is hearing around him.

He knows intuitively that there are some words that behave like verbs, and others like nouns, and that there is a limited set of possibilities as to their ordering within a phrase.

This is information which is never taught directly to him by the adults that surround him. It is simply there in his environment.

By observing what others say and how they say it he works out how to speak for himself.

This ability, which is part of his human inheritance, is what Chomsky calls the 'Language Acquisition Device.'

I think that when Chomsky refers to a child 'intuitively' knowing that there are some words that behave like verbs and others like nouns, that he is describing the same learning process as described in Mcnamara's theory of language.

Mcnamara believes that a child first reads the meaning of a situation, and then works out the relationship between the words he hears spoken and the actions or response which accompany them.

Chapter 27

Growing Demands On The Child's Language

Children deduce, or work out for themselves, the agreed word order in their community. They are not formally taught grammar. They 'acquire' it. So with from a small number of words, using `some rules', they can create a vast number of sentences. The result of this, is that once a child can master these rules and transformations, he has the ability to create and expand on his grammar by using these rules to create new sentences that he has not heard before. This is shown in the great deal of creativity which occurs in a child's grammatical utterances.

So what evidence is there to support Chomsky's view of 'transformational generative grammar'; and that the 'language acquisition device' is an innate biological 'species specific' human characteristic?

All languages of the world share similar characteristics of using nouns, verbs, pronouns, though not necessarily in a similar order.

Grammar and complex language usage seem also to be a `uniquely human capability' as no other species on the planet seems to possess such proficiency as humans.

Chomsky, sees language as coming more from criteria *inside* the child's mind, rather than – Skinner's idea of it – being an imitation of adult speech, coming from o*utside* the child's mind. Indeed Chomsky took Skinner very much to task not only for this, but for many other aspects of his work, such as for example, saying that children's speech mistakes are corrected.

Chomsky said that they weren't.

But in fact if you look at the situation closely enough both men are correct.

Indeed Chomsky in his strong criticism of Skinner very nearly threw out the baby with the bath water!

Chomsky is correct in that the *very earliest* utterances are accepted by adults and go uncorrected in any way, as with Erin and her 'bay' for 'bear'. But it isn't long before the parental attitude shifts somewhat. This is because as adults, rearing a child to be ultimately independent, they are still – however unconsciously – operating the same teaching principles I outlined earlier in the building brick scenario. That is, they are always presenting the child with tasks a little beyond where he is now, but equally with targets he can achieve. That is, they work, as Vygotsky would say, within the child's zone of proximal development.

Piaget echoes this parental shifting of the goals when he describes how he believes a child's intellectual growth occurs.

He compares it to what happens when you climb a ladder. You get a different view from each step up you take. So each new concept the child discovers gives him an added view of the world and how it works. How children see things at any stage is the result of their current knowledge.

For example initially, Mum is 'the one who looks after him'. That is her role in life, full stop. Then through time it dawns on him that when mum is in her office she is also doing another kind of work. As his original perception of mum as solely his minder changes to take in this new view of her, his understanding of her role broadens and he has moved up a step on the ladder to get another, different view of reality.

He has changed, or adapted, his first understanding to accommodate his new knowledge. Each change, or accommodation, of new information takes him a further step up the ladder.

Parents or caretakers seem to understand these shifts in perspective and adapt their own behaviour to the child, so that their demands match his growing intellect.

So are language mistakes not corrected?

As I wrote earlier Erin's initial half words and single word sentences were totally accepted, understood as far as possible, and responded to as if they were fully correct forms of human speech.

Time changed this quite significantly.

For instance at the age of 3.4 in the space of *less than 20 minutes* I heard Erin corrected *four* times by her dad for what he saw as errors in her speech. Some of their dialogue went like this;

'I'm going to a par'y.'
'No Erin you are going to a par*t*y. Say party.'
'I'm going to a party.'
'Grandma Helen I want some milk now.'
'No Erin. Say, "Grandma Helen could I have some milk please."'
'Can I have some milk Grandma Helen please?'

Even the way she now addresses me as 'Grandma Helen', rather than just 'Helen' is another result of her father's teaching. He believed that calling me by my first name was not appropriate at her young age!

These corrections, and many more similar, all seem to be of pronunciation, or of socially acceptable manners of speech. They are not so much corrections of language, but corrections of how you *use* language. In this sense Skinner is one hundred per cent correct.

Parents are using language as a tool to regulate behaviour.

But they are still intuitively operating within Vygotsky's ZPD.

That is, they have adapted their initial acceptance of mistakes to take account of the child's increasing competence with language, and they now make corrections because the child is capable of understanding and learning from these corrections; whereas too early correction would have simply gone over the child's head, and wasted the adult's energy.

Chapter 28

Learning To Read

Once a child's *spoken* vocabulary is up and running, and they are communicating easily with those around them, many parents start to think of teaching the child to read. They realise that in the contemporary world a child needs to be literate. This will facilitate formal schooling and immeasurably speed up an individual child's learning.

Many people ask how can I teach my child to read?

Educational research shows that good teaching of reading depends on three factors.

1. The teacher knows what he is teaching.
2. The teacher understands how learning takes place.
3. The teacher has teaching skill.

Let's go through these factors one at a time.

1. *The teacher knows what he is teaching.*

Well this is really obvious if you think about it for a bit. When your child learned to talk, you probably didn't much consciously teach, but you knew the meaning of the words you were using. So, yes, equally when you are teaching reading you will know the meaning of the words you use. More important you will know exactly which words your child uses and understands. You will use these words in your own unique reading scheme.

2. *The teacher understands how learning takes place.*
You may feel that you are on less firm ground here, but don't worry. Because you are not going to teach *formally*. There is going to be no hint of an old fashioned schoolmaster or schoolmistress in a Victorian classroom. You may not have noticed what you did teaching spoken language, so I am going to remind you of the major facts covered earlier and see how they apply to reading skills.

For now it is enough for me to tell you that if your child is talking you can teach. Because the child has learned this skill from you!

And more comforting than that, to someone who is nervous of teaching a child to read, is the fact that more and more reception and early class rooms are trying as far as possible to imitate the learning atmosphere of the home! Even in many forward thinking secondary schools there is a move towards recognising that a teacher is much more effective when they do not formally and directly teach.

The best learning seems to take place when the teacher provides a situation within which learning can take place.

The teacher becomes more of a facilitator of learning, a consultant in the classroom, ready to answer questions as and when they arise. Just like Mums and Dads do automatically all the time. In the modern classroom a sign of really active learning is when the pupil questions the teacher more than vice versa. The pupils who are as involved in classroom tasks as they were earlier in play make the best progress. If the best teachers are recognising more and more the that the best learning copies the way the preschool child learns then the conclusion is obvious –

3. *You have teaching skill!*
We now do understand how a child learns to speak. You have read what elements are involved in the earlier pages and understand much of the process. This knowledge will help you to teach your child to read. I will describe a very simple method to you, and the logic behind it, and you will soon realise that it is really quite easy once you understand a few principles.

This method I have designed for use by adults who want to show children under five how to learn to read. It is meant to be fun both for the child and adult. It is not a chore. And you are in a unique position to do this teaching supremely well. This is because the more we understand and use a *child's own experience* as a basis for learning the better the learning will be.

Learning To Read

You have already proved yourself to be a superb language teacher by teaching your child how to talk!

As I wrote earlier, all five year olds starting school can talk. They could just as easily be reading if the person caring for them had the knowledge to show them how!

You need first to spend some time looking back at the factors which enabled your child to learn to speak. It will be these same factors you will now more consciously use when you help your child to learn to read.

The idea behind this method is that it uses the way a child naturally learns spoken words to let the child learn written words. This method will be unique to each individual child, though obviously it will share many common characteristics with other schemes. In my experience as a parent, teacher and grandparent I have seen it work. I know because I used it years ago to teach my own children, and later grand children, to read.

Obviously I have refined and reviewed my ideas down the years, always conscious of the possibility of improvements. But once you are clear that it is the placing of work (or rather play!) just a little tiny bit beyond where the child is now you have understand how the deepest learning takes place.

Moreover, this method is practical, taking a common sense – and low-cost! – approach to learning. I am frequently aggravated when I see remarkably expensive books and toys advertised as developing your child's skills in this or that way, when very often a little imagination and creativity on the part of a parent could be equally, if not more, successful. Maybe it is a commercial ploy, playing on a parent's very natural wish to do their best for their child, which encourages the conclusion that the more money you spend the more advantages your child will have.

I actually saw the almost unbelievable. This was in a lavishly produced and consequently pricey, book of First Words for a toddler. One of the words was 'secateurs'! I ask you how many toddlers have 'secateurs' as part of their everyday vocabulary? Before that I thought the 'xylophone' we had as children in our ABC was the worst example of inappropriate vocabulary for a child I had come across.

When your baby was small, and still just babbling, you made a big effort to get him to talk. Remember all that 'Motherese'? You used talk he could attend to in order to promote his own speech.

This is very probably why one of the best ways to teach your child to read is quite simply

– *Read to your child*!

The Language Barrier

All the teaching professionals agree that this is a major factor in developing reading skill. So from very early on, even before the child is talking, read to him.

Talk about the story, perhaps chat about the pictures. Have fun, knowing in the back of your mind that you are helping the child understand lots about reading. The child will see how you hold a book, how you turn pages, how you start at the front of the book and finish at the back. When they are ready and have learned to lift a book, turn it the right way up, and turn pages, they will play at reading.

The wording used in the book will also help develop their spoken language skills, as very often the narrative is expressed in a way that we rarely use in every day chat with a child.

Once a child is talking we can take it for granted that he now recognises that separate distinct sounds have a particular meaning. So it is much easier for him to recognise that the letters of the alphabet also can each have a different sound.

The written form of a sound is easier to grasp possibly than his first realisation that special sounds have individual meanings. So in a way the concept of reading is going to be easier for him to grasp now that he has already worked out the concept of talk.

Now just suppose we want the child to understand that letter shapes can have meaning. It seems logical to go about this opening of the child's mind to reading in a manner as closely replicating 'sound has meaning' as possible.

Chapter 29

The Sense Of Sight In A Child

Hearing opened the world of speech, because adults provided the correct 'scaffolding'.

That is:

Caretakers gave the child a constant opportunity to hear words spoken in a way that was of interest to the child.

Read frequently to the child, books which are of interest to him.

Reading aloud to a child mimics the one sided conversations you held earlier with him when he was learning to talk. His first books are picture books with illustrations of a world he recognises. Just as turn taking in conversation and the 'conventions' of talk are shown in one sided conversations so now opening the book, turning the pages, reaching the end, the conventions of reading are being learned.

They used tones and pitch which he could hear and respond to.

Use books with very large print and plentiful illustrations.

Discuss the story. Talk about the pictures as well as reading the text.

They used speech in situations which the child was enjoying. He was playing.

Reading should be done where the child is comfortable and relaxed. This could be bedtime, or daytime, on a couch or armchair.

The richer the quality and variety of play the more language he listened to.

The greater variety of text he hears and illustration he sees the more he will want to read for himself.

They didn't get upset by his initial 'failure' or 'mistakes'.

Even learning to turn pages one at a time is quite a feat for a child. Be patient and he will get there eventually!

They also used language as a useful tool in their everyday life.

Make clear to your child how useful reading is to you. Your child got very speedy at talking once he realised that words work to make life easier. Remember that 'naming explosion'! Even when a child can't read it helps their understanding of reading if they can see for themselves how useful it is to you in daily life.

There are many situations where we read and never mention the fact to a child. Perhaps we should try now and then to make it clear what it is we are doing by reading aloud. You already read aloud at story time, but it's not this I mean. It's when you look at a map for directions, or check signs in a shop or supermarket for the location of things you want or to see what special offers the shop has this week. Very often we do this silently, and don't say to the child how we got our information.

Maybe we look up the time of a programme on television, read our morning post, read e mails, text messages, or look for the ingredients for a recipe. Talk about what you are doing so the child sees that reading has many uses. Show the child how you use reading. You don't obviously have to do this every time you read. But if you even only very occasionally do so the child will quite quickly see the advantages of being a reader.

Nobody once thought too much about *teaching* the child to speak. Talking was a part of normal everyday life. They just created the right environment for speech to emerge itself. If you replicate this atmosphere with reading the child will soon be asking, 'Can I do some reading?'

As I noted before hearing opened the world of speech. Now think about this in relation to reading. Sight can now open the world of reading. The child is already using spoken words and just needs the correct scaffolding to understand written words. So just as adult speech was adjusted to suit the stage of development in the hearing and comprehension level of the child, so the reading materials in this method should be printed to match the level of competence of young eyes. Let's take a look at what researchers have discovered in this field.

The visual system is the least developed of all the senses in infancy. This is because the 'hardware', so to speak, which makes up the visual system is not fully developed at birth. The muscles which guide the movements of the eyes need time to mature.

This is probably why a well fed infant who is a bit drowsy tends to look a bit drunk! Equally the cells of the retina need more time before they can function properly. As well, the parts of the brain which process information from the eyes, and the pathways themselves that this information will travel along need time to mature.

This means that very young children cannot see normal size print as easily as older children and it is why the first materials you use should be printed very large. In fact it should be at least

this size – if not

bigger!

In fact it is estimated that print for children between two and four years of age needs to be at least one inch high. Under twos need two and a half inch sized letters if they are to focus with any accuracy on their shape! As the child's visual skills and memory of shape develop the print can be smaller, but it will still be large by adult standards.

A clear preference for human faces is in evidence by 3 months of age. By observing and recording how babies examine the face much useful information was gained. Apart from learning that young babies prefer very sharp contrast, like black against white, studies of infant perception show that initially infants scan the outer part of a picture of a face and later fill in the details.

If the early drawings of children are any evidence to go by, then this filling in from the face outwards continues for quite a while. Three and four year olds all tend to draw pictures of themselves and mummy and daddy. These show people with huge circular heads, two small circles for eyes, a blob for nose and often a big semi circle of a smile. The body is totally missed out, though gradually four stick like lines emerge from the head to indicate arms and legs. This is definitely focussing on the essentials, and ignoring the rest!

So it seems logical to suppose that a child will see whole words first before they break each word down into the individual letters used to write it. This kind of reading where a child recognises a word by its complete shape is called 'Look Say' or 'Sight' reading. Just as in their drawings they still do not seem to register the full word, just some outer clue to its meaning.

At 4.9 for example, Erin read 'bag' as 'bar'. Of course using phonic sounds can be helpful as well as Look Say in the early stages of reading. When I pointed out to Erin that it was a 'guh' not 'reh' sounding letter she read 'bag' correctly. So it appears that if a child knows both the conventional alphabet, *and* the phonic alphabet, this will be a great help to progress.

Phonics are used to encourage a child to sound out the letters to work out the meaning of a written word. But to my mind this is a passing scaffolding stage in reading. Certainly I don't now find myself sounding out words when I read. So a useful tool at an early learning stage but finally unnecessary when the fluent reader is back to totally Look Say. Besides there comes a stage when reading vocabulary demands more than the simple sound equivalent of each letter.

(It's amusing to note that the word 'phonic' itself is not phonic!)

Say a child has come across a word new to him in reading. He tries sounding it out but that doesn't work.

'Eh el eh peh heh ah neh the' – doesn't sound like any word he already knows.

So he asks for help. You look at it and see 'elephant', so you say 'elephant'.

Now unless you choose early words very carefully you could find yourself too early on trying to explain that consonant clusters affect sound in a different way to when the consonants are used singly. You can't even use the term consonant cluster as very likely they have no idea what either of the two words mean!

This is a bit much for a very young child. Remember the child was slower to get to these in talk as well. If at an early stage you are asked about a word like this I think it is best to explain that some words are 'funny' and don't follow the usual rules. That when you get p and h together they sound like f.

Erin at 4.8 was quite agreeable to accept the waywardness of some words like this. For example one day, to label a drawing she had done, she asked me to spell 'left' and 'right.'

I did so and she accepted 'left' without comment; but when I spelled out 'right' for her, she said, 'That doesn't look like right, does it Grandma?' I agreed with her and just said that some words were like that, they didn't look at all like they sounded. She accepted that as enough explanation.

Chapter 30

Games To Help Early Reading

It is valuable, long before a child shows an interest in reading for himself, to have a poster of the alphabet, with very large lettering, permanently on a wall in a room where the child often plays. This gets him familiar with the shapes of letters. The letters of the alphabet after all are going to be for the child the elements of reading just as babbling provided the elements of speech to the infant. When he asks about the poster you tell him that it is the 'alphabet' and that it shows all the 'letters' we use in reading and writing. He is now learning the vocabulary of reading with the words 'alphabet' and 'letters'. These tools now become valued playthings in lots of games.

He will probably have bricks with similar letters that he plays with. You might offer to show him the letter his name begins with. If he is interested you could then write out – in BIG script – all the letters needed to spell this name. You can easily buy very large tip black markers which make this task easier for you. Since it is very interesting to himself, his name, he will probably be quite happy with this.

You can then reinforce this information casually in many play times and routines. Make his food on his plate, – chips, peas, bread fingers are all good foods for 'writing' – spell his name or initial. You can make biscuits cut out in letter shapes. He is tasting the alphabet!

He can make play dough letters. He can sign his paintings or label 'Mummy' and 'Daddy' in his drawings. He can be the first to spot 'T' for Tesco, or 'M' for McDonalds when you go shopping, and so on. There are

The Language Barrier

numerous ways to play with the alphabet once you start to look for such opportunities.

Another game Erin enjoyed at this stage was 'drawing letters on her back.' For this you need to have the child facing away from you and with your fingertip trace the outline of a large capital letter on his back. So not only is the child seeing, hearing, tasting letters, he is also feeling them physically. And none of this is work. It is all games you are playing together.

It is very important that you do play lots of games and that the child has a wide range of concrete experiences of letters and their sounds before you attempt reading.

When he decides that he wants to read, or when you feel that he is ready, write his name on a piece of card like a plain postcard, again in BIG letters. Include two other similar cards with 'Mummy' and 'Daddy' written on them in the same style. Now the game is to say which is which. Have a sturdy box like a shoe box or similar to store these cards in after play. Because you are now going to build up his reading vocabulary, slowly, bit by bit.

When learning to talk, as I have already mentioned earlier, there is what is known as the 'silent period'. This is the name for the time when a child's silent, or unspoken vocabulary will be far greater than the 'surface', or 'productive' vocabulary. That is to say parents are often aware of words which the child obviously knows but is not as yet himself using in his own speech. Research in language shows that it takes an average of *five months* for a child, who has shown that they can understand a word, to produce that word themselves in speech.

This is important when thinking about learning to read. The learner will need great exposure to letters and written words before the learning will actually become internalised and produce a result.

Remember when your child learned to speak you constantly modelled language of the here and now. Equally here you are now modelling reading, using the familiar everyday language of the child. So choose new reading words to add to his postcard game with this in mind. To help you with this you might want to again refer back to what happens when a child is learning to talk. The lists of the first fifty words spoken words by a child offer really valuable insights into how we should select words for our own unique reading scheme for beginners.

1. In the early stages pick short words with no consonant clusters.
2. Words like 'baby', 'mummy', 'daddy' are useful with the repetition of sounds.

GAMES TO HELP EARLY READING

Children love rhyme, rhythm and repetition. I think that this is the key to the continuing success of the Dr. Suess early reading books, like 'The Cat in the Hat', or 'Fox in Socks.'

3. Pick words which begin with the consonants research shows appear first in a child's speech. These are b, f, k, n, p, d, g, m, and h. Examples are bat, pin, man and so on.

4. Choose words that end in b, f, k, n, p. Such as mop, which would led to hop, top, and so on.

5. Choose words that the child already uses correctly in speech.

6. Choose mainly nouns.

Short three letter words are best to begin with. From Erin's early list I for example choose bad, bag, bed, car, hat and so on. When introducing these to her – very slowly, the work spread over a lot of time, – I would say things like, 'This word is bed.' and show her 'bed' written on a postcard.

'It starts with the letter b' – pointing to it – 'which makes a beh sound. Beh beh beh sound. Let's see if we can think of any other word that starts with the same beh sound. I know! Let's find things this week that begin with a beh sound. Ball. Ball could be one. Ball begins with beh.'

A second point to note about these very early words is that they are all or mostly – apart from perhaps family names – phonic. That is to say if the child knows the sound the letter makes in reading then he will be able to build the three sounds to make the word written in front of him.

At the end of about a week in small bursts of this play, looking at the four cards already made, and playing the game of which word is which, we might select our best b for 'beh' word we found during the week. This happens when you notice something in the child's environment and point the letter out by sounding it.

'It's a nice fine day for bat and ball games in the garden. Bat, ball, they're two beh sounds! Beh-at! Beh-all!

Or at bath time, 'Let's make some bubbles in the bath. Hey! Bubbles! Bath! They're two more 'beh' words!'

You will find that just by being occasionally aware of the need to locate words starting with the letter b that you will have at least ten or more listed. At this time if you make use of the free magazines that nowadays most of the large supermarkets regularly provide free for customers you have a rich source of pictures of items beginning with your week's letter.

The child can cut these out, or you can, and then paste or glue them to a large sheet of paper. You provide the labelling for each item. Children enjoy cutting and pasting, and you are in no way formally teaching.

Nevertheless the child is 'soaking in' the letter b and the sound it makes! Continue in this fashion to build up your postcard game vocabulary.

You can if you prefer use a loose leaf file, and stick the picture and words in, each on a separate page with BIG print labelling, to make your child's own unique reading scheme. 'Wow! We are writing a book!'

But do remember that the child first spoke in one word sentences. Your initial sentences must also be of the one word type. Like have a picture of a dog and the writing 'dog'.

Learning to read must be fun, enjoyable, with material very, very carefully selected to match the child's interests, abilities and level of vocabulary.

If I didn't like the feeling of not always understanding the sounds Erin was making in the early days of her speech – it is actually quite frustrating when this happens with a young child – I could not then later expect her to enjoy struggling to understand the symbols for words she was seeing. And just as the environment and context provided clues to the meaning of sounds at an early stage of learning to talk, so now the pictures provide the necessary clue to the meaning of words when reading.

You always select words to use which are already in your child's spoken vocabulary. You then use this as one of the child's reading books, just as you would any other, but now you have the satisfaction of knowing that you are reading words ideally matched to your child's level of development. They have worked hard to learn how to articulate a word, and, now that they can do it, you set the next target; looking at it in print until one magical day they will recognise it without the contextual clue!

These are also those words which are familiar to your child in his own unique environment. This might be a photo of a brother or sister, or a special pet, or whatever really, or a picture cut from a magazine which shows what you want to name, labelled by you following the size and style of lettering used in the rest of the folder. For each word you put in the folder make a postcard copy for your word game box. The game is now growing and developing with the child, and when he plays he is attempting to read words out of context. This is quite hard to do.

But if you proceed slowly, with only one word or two a week added, it will soon grow to fifty or so. Now the same as in speech, you have a sizeable foundation to build on. Just as the 'naming explosion' occurs in speaking, so a reading 'explosion' can follow now.

Chapter 31

An Analysis of Early Reading Steps

Remember Chomsky pointing out that children are able to deduce general rules from particular instance of speech? They start to work out rules for themselves. It can also be so in reading, especially if you give a few nudges in the right direction. For example, say they can read 'cat' as one of their first fifty postcards. So you can now introduce bat, hat, rat, sat and so on. They will understand these words much more quickly when you point out that the similar 'at' in all of them.

The child has built up a set of letters whose consonant and vowel sounds he knows how to read. He maximises these to pick up new words. For example, as I wrote earlier, Erin could say 'cap' (meaning clap); she could also say 'up', wanting to be lifted up. So she had the skills of making the word 'cup', without as much effort and practise as the original two words took her.

So it is with reading.

Perhaps the child recognises the word 'car' so now bar, far, jar, and so on can be added in to the word box and be recognised far more quickly now that the 'ar' sound has been learned.

Soon the child will have enough basic reading vocabulary to want to start reading to you! I find it best to suggest that we *share* the reading.

An example of this from Erin at 4.10. We were sharing reading an amusingly illustrated account of 'the big bad wolf'. Each time we came to the phrase 'the big bad wolf' Erin read. Sometimes words were beyond her like 'fierce'. Without breaking the rhythm of the story telling I would say the unknown word and she read the rest of the sentence. So if *italics* are my words and the rest Erin's it would go like this.

'The big bad wolf *arrived* at the home of the *first* of the three little pigs.' The 'three little pigs' is deduced from the illustration and we have met the phrase a few times already earlier in the text.

At this stage she could *almost* read (carefully selected books to match her reading ability), on her own but really enjoyed tackling more difficult stories like this, where we shared the actual reading. She would scan each page in advance and say, 'You can read that and that,' and point to words she knew she didn't know. 'I will read the rest.'

Now all of this might seem at first like a lot of hard work for you.

But it is not.

Look at it this way – if you weren't playing reading with the child, the child would either be bored and a start being a nuisance, or you would be entertaining the child in some other way. There may be days and even weeks when you do very little, but just being *aware* of how you can help the child to read will be of enormous benefit, to you *both*. For example you are going on a longish – for a child – car journey. You hear the whinge, 'How long *more* before we get there?'

You can easily distract the child's boredom by playing a reading game. I Spy something beginning with letter c, the sound cuh or whatever. Then you could play, 'Let's see how many words we know beginning with an 'f' for 'feh' sound. I'll say one and then you say one and the loser is whoever stops first.'

You not only prevent a childish session of whining you reinforce reading skills. I am sure you can think of many more 'games' yourself!

Around this stage of reading your child will probably have started in a School Reception class, and soon will be bringing home little reading books to go through as a homework. Show the child that you love listening to these stories – even if you regard it as a chore! – asking things like, 'Did you get a good story to read to me today?'

Remember when the child was learning to talk he often spoke aloud to himself. Now equally he needs to hear himself read aloud so he understands through hearing as well as vision.

According to his biographers the great American president, Abraham Lincoln, even as an adult, *always* read aloud! He is described as having great concentration and when he wished to read he did so, shutting out of his consciousness everything, and indeed everyone, around him. When he was asked about this behaviour he replied,

An Analysis of Early Reading Steps

"When I read aloud, two senses catch the idea: first, I see what I read; second, I hear it, and therefore I can remember it better."
This effect of reading aloud is equally valuable to a child.

And don't forget that children in the early stages of talking go through stages of repeated babbling, often followed by later constant repetitions of single or two word strings for quite a while. They have to practise these new skills to get them right! That is another reason to encourage your child with the reading books they start to bring home from school. These will be carefully graded to the reading ability of the child. They will initially include one word sentences, then proceed to short almost telegraphic sentences with again lots of repeated vocabulary.

You now understand why this is! They are following the pattern of learning to talk.

If you have been playing sorting and classifying games with your child this will be of immense help to him in the next stage of learning to read, because pure phonic letters as such are going to let him down!

Sort bricks by colour
Sort cutlery by type
Sort buttons by size/colour /number of holes.
Sort food shopping for fridge, freezer or cupboard.
Sort ironing for where the clothes are to go.
Sort leaves by size.
Sort pastas by shape............and so on.

These types of game and activities are not only invaluable for building a great maths foundation, but also for learning to read.

Learning the *names* of each letter was the first step.
Learning the *sounds* of the letters came next.
Learning to sound out short, usually three letter words came next.

The next stage is learning that the same letters can have *different* sounds depending on their context – or in the child's experience – how they are sorted.

This presupposes that the child has developed cognitive skills from actually experiencing for himself that how you sort things can change in different ways while the things which you are sorting stay the same.

Buttons in a box stay buttons whether they are sorted by colour, size or number of holes.

Take for example, the two letters 'a' and 't'. In 'hat' these are sounded phonetically, but this is not so in 'ate'. The presence of the 'e' alters the sound. But since we know that now this child is capable of classifying, and also of making particular instances of language lead to the formulation of general rules, then when you introduce a word like this with an 'ate' sound, he will more quickly learn if you then add in date, gate, late and so fairly rapidly, compared to his initial learning of letters and sounds, build up a reading vocabulary.

Obviously, the *first* instance of change of sound will be harder for the child to comprehend than the next, and then later ones. However, as you gradually go back to the three letter phonics he has learned by now and develop them to longer four letter words he will grasp the idea.

Similarly, the 'a' and 'r' of earlier words like 'bar' can develop into the different 'ar' sound in 'bare' , and then you add care, dare, and so on. If you proceed like this, looking at his three letter word reading vocabulary, and progressively altering it to four letter rhyming vocabulary, you will be starting the reading explosion similar to the 'naming explosion'.

And one final word here.

A child learning to speak goes through a phase of pointing at things and asking. 'What's that?'

Adults usually respond with the name of the object in question without hesitation.

However, the same adult for some reason I cannot fathom, when asked by a child learning to read, 'What's this word?' will more likely reply with, 'Have you tried to sound it out? Sound it out bit by bit and see if you can work out what it is.'

Why?

The child has tried to read the word already and obviously can't decipher it. He has asked for help so at least give it.

Suppose the word is 'carpet'.

Tell him carpet; and then get in some kind of 'sounding out' message if you want.

'Oh! Look. It's car and pet! That's funny! We don't have a car and a pet on our floor do we?'

If it is a shorter word, spelt phonetically, then having given the word to the child, you could say something like, 'I sounded out the letters. It's leh, eh, geh, so leg!'

The child (who you remember in acquiring speech is capable of deducing general rules from particular instances) will equally learn deciphering techniques in reading.

Chapter 32

Moving On To Writing

Now my attitude to reading is not at all in line with current teaching methods if a sheet of advice to parents helping a child learn to read is anything to go by. Erin brought it home from school at age 5.8.

I'll quote from it for you:-

"To help your child tackle problem words you can ask these questions:

- What does the word begin with?
- What does the word end with?
- What sound is in the middle?
- If all else fails, does looking at the picture help?
- Try reading on, missing out the problem word, then going back to it."

Quite frankly, in my opinion, this advice is anticipating multiple failures on the part of the child. You would have tried three separate clues before realising that *'all else fails'* (including the child) requires you to use a fourth. Then a fifth which still does not tell the child what he wants to know.

Now if you think I exaggerate here imagine you have just bought a new high technology gadget, say a digital camera. You have some knowledge of how such cameras work, and you know that a friend of yours uses one quite expertly. This camera includes some functions you have never met with before so you ask your friend to explain to you how they operate. You are very keen to become as expert as him.

Your friend does not tell you.

Instead he gives a clue.
Still you don't understand, so you get another clue.
Still not there so you get another clue.
And another.

Still you are unenlightened. So your friend very kindly says, 'I will use other functions on the camera and later come back to this. Maybe by then you will have worked it out for yourself!'

I really don't think you are going to feel very happy about this style of 'help.'

Sometime in this process the child will want to start writing. He will maybe want to sign his own name on a greeting card or similar. Once he begins to show an interest you quite obviously encourage this in games and play. You also let him see you using writing for different purposes. These could be writing a shopping list, a letter, a telephone message to pass to someone else and so on.

'Do you want to draw a Birthday card for daddy? Do you want to write happy birthday on it?' This kind of writing is seen by the child to have a purpose and not just a job to be done. They scarcely realise that they are learning to write because their attention is focussed on the purpose of their efforts.

Vygotsky wrote very well on this topic. He said,

'... teaching should be organized in such a way that reading and writing are *necessary for something*. If they are used only to write official greetings to the staff or whatever the teacher thinks up (and clearly suggests to them), then the exercise will be purely mechanical and may soon bore the child; his activity will not be manifest in his writing and his budding personality will not grow. Reading and writing must be something the child needs ... writing must be "*relevant to life*" – in the same way that we require a "relevant" arithmetic.'

(The italics are mine.)

After all the things you learn as a grown up are what you *want* to learn. How to do your job efficiently, how to drive a car, how to cook, how to have a garden. We become quite expert at these and other things because we *want* to.

A child who is encouraged in this way soon gets quite ambitious in writing, and will ask for help with spellings. Mistakes will occur of course, but very often they reveal where a child is slightly mispronouncing a spoken word and this shows up in the way he spells the word. For example, Erin in a piece of early writing said that she put on her 'bjamas' going to bed. She wrote 'poply' for 'properly', 'in joyd' for 'enjoyed' and sometimes we needed a cryptologist skill to decipher her meanings.

Pizzas became 'peesus', new clothes were 'noo clos', a watch 'woch', but following the pattern of adult behaviour in early speech development no one commented on these creative spellings, just tried gallantly to decipher them when she gave us a letter or a story! However her correctly spelt words also increased steadily as she asked for spellings of words when she wrote a piece for one reason or another.

Besides 'mistakes' are often useful for pointing out to the adult which spoken words need reinforcement in their correct form. For instance Erin wrote a bot for about, and better still, 'a mergensy' for emergency. There is also the possibility that words for which the child requests a spelling may be more easily recognised in future when the child encounters them in reading. So by encouraging writing you are reinforcing both speaking and reading skills!

Of course reading is essential to develop language even more than a child usually would if they just used spoken words. In books they will meet with new vocabulary, and sentences more structured than those we tend to use in every day life.

Chomsky in particular remarks on the fragmented way we use speech in daily life, hesitating, back tracking, repeating words or phrases and altering our minds as we go on. If a child is to really know the correct forms of language he will need reading to give him better samples of it then he would get from listening to talk only.

Chapter 33

Children Acquire Culture Through Language

I noticed that that when Erin was three years old and really getting fluent in her talk that she often went on from one particular incident to create a general rule for behaviour.

For instance back from an outing where the family had a pre-dinner drink in the hotel bar, she asked me did I like wine. I said that I did. So she told me, 'At home grandmas drink tea. When they go to a bar they drink wine because ladies drink wine in bars. My mum drinks wine. Daddies drink beer and children drink water.'

So because she had seen a particular kind of behaviour in one setting she then generalised it to include the whole world. This is very similar to the child's thought processes earlier when he over extended some words, such as because the adult male in his house was 'daddy', all adult males are 'daddy'. The adults in Erin's family behaved in a certain way *one* evening; from that she deduced that *all* parents and grand parents worldwide behaved in a similar manner *all the time*.

Similarly, another day she was going shopping with her dad. He said, 'Come on Erin. Let's get your shoes on. We're going shopping.'

The next day she told me, 'Children don't go shopping without shoes on. No.'

This moving from the particular to the general for rules of behaviour seems to be very similar to Chomsky's description of language acquisition.

Remember he noticed that, 'Children do not simply copy the language that they hear around them. They *deduce rules from it*, which they can then use to produce sentences that they have never heard before.'

The really significant point made here is that children *deduce rules* from small instances of language. This individual rule is then applied and tested on a much wider field to see how far their idea or hypothesis concerning usage is correct.

For example the 'mistakes' they frequently make in speech are caused when they extend a rule to where it does not apply. Such as, 'I runned really fast.'

Though on balance in every day life, the extension is usually correct; and their speech and ability to communicate develops very rapidly. We notice and smile at their errors because they are unusual, not because they are the norm.

And because they *do* make such errors then it must be that they are applying a general rule to a particular situation where it does not fit. If they are doing so then they must have at some stage formulated for themselves such a general rule.

No one has sat them down and directly taught them any rules of grammar. They have worked it for themselves. The only adult assistance has to be that they are the everyday providers of speech in mother tongue, which the child must then use as material for thought.

I would suggest that not only do children go from the particular to the general *in language*; but that they use the same technique in every learning situation in every sphere of life.

Chomsky said that they had an innate LAD. It can be seen most clearly in the overextensions they make first in speech, then in reading.

From my observations of children I would go much further and suggest that what they have is an innate ability to form general rules from the particular; be it language, behaviour, a routine, whatever.

In one sense a child's speech is merely a way in which their thought processes can be made evident.

The ability to deduce an overall rule from isolated incidents does *not* operate *solely* in the field of language. The child who hears daddy say, 'Put your shoes on we're going out,' learns that you wear shoes when you go outdoors.

When mummy says, 'Wash your hands we are going to eat,' the child abstracts people wash their hands before eating. And so on.

Observe young children and you will see this replicated time after time.

The Language Barrier

Thus not only language *but the behaviour or culture* of the group is absorbed by the child. By culture I mean that which is correct behaviour, or acceptable, within a group of people.

Children constantly try to replicate familiar situations. If they have been to a birthday party where there is a cake and candles then every birthday must be celebrated in the same way. If you buy them sweets in a shop then the next time you visit the same shop they will expect sweets again whether or not you had intended buying them.

They are startled when a routine changes. They laugh at the unexpected.

But, even more importantly, at this stage not only are they learning language, but through language they are generalising to create the rules of behaviour acceptable in their community.

Here is a scene, a version of which I am sure that at some time you have seen yourself.

Two quite young children are playing, let's say, on a beach. They are Mary who is four and Michael who is one year older. They are quite happily engaged in building sand castles until suddenly Mary stands up and walks on one of Michael's castles. Michael is infuriated and immediately hits Mary quite hard on the head with his plastic spade. Mary is hurt and full of indignation, and runs screaming to her Mother who is sitting nearby.

'Mummy! Mummy! Michael hit me on the head!'

Mother soothes Mary, saying, 'Poor Mary! Let me rub it better for you! But you really should try to be more careful and not walk on Michael's castles.'

She calls Michael.

'Michael you are *not* to hit Mary! I know she walked on one of your castles, but you can always build it again. Besides she's your little sister, and you should take care of her, and not hit her. Boys don't hit girls, and especially do not hit their own sister! Now Mary you say, "Sorry" to Michael for knocking his castle; and Michael you say, "Sorry" to Mary for hitting her. Then both of you go back and play nicely'.

End of one story.

Now backtrack to where Mary is screaming, 'Mummy! Mummy! Michael hit me on the head!'

This time a different, but equally recognisable scene, occurs.

Mother stands up exasperated.

'Stop that yelling Mary! You're giving me quite a headache. I'm sick of you running to me every time you and Michael have a fight. What have I told you?

If he hits you, you hit him back! Sort out your own battles! If the pair of you fight again I'll take you straight home. Now go and play and leave me alone!'

End of second story.

You will see that in each example Mother uses speech to guide behaviour. But in the two versions the children are offered very different rules.

In one, *despite the blatant evidence to the contrary*, which both children have been closely involved in, Mother states as if it were a law of nature, that 'Boys do not hit girls.' Neither child ever argues this point! They accept the ruling, and return to play. Language here has already become more powerful than actions.

In the second instance, the children learn that fighting is quite permissible; indeed it is recommended – as long as the adults are not disturbed.

In this way, through language, children become encultured into the rules and expected behaviours of their own particular social groups.

When as adults we say things like,

'Everybody knows......' or

'It's only common sense that...'

we are usually not aware that what we perceive to be 'what everybody knows' or 'common sense' is, in fact, only our own, deeply ingrained since childhood, ways of seeing the world.

When unexpectedly, or suddenly, we come across views diametrically opposed to our own we are very often struck quite dumb with the shock.

'I was speechless!'

'I didn't know what to say!'

'I was dumbstruck!'

Because we have absorbed behaviour rules so unconsciously with language we are quite literally lost for words when our viewpoint is suddenly or unexpectedly challenged.

I think this is how children make sense of their world, how they work out what are the rules which govern acceptable behaviour in their family and community. They observe or take part in an incident, and from that one instance devise a general rule for such situations. In other words they learn their community's culture.

Culture can be defined as any system of shared beliefs and values, customs and behaviours, that a group of people use to cope with their world and with one another. This culture is transmitted from generation to generation through learning. And significantly the learning takes place through language.

That people *learn* their culture is an essential part of any definition of the word. It is not transmitted genetically, like for example, the infant's need for food. On the other hand an adult's desire for a *specific* food may be a learned cultural response to a physiological feeling of hunger.

So culture is then that which is perceived as good or bad, what is acceptable and what is not, what is enjoyable; in *every* aspect of daily life. Most importantly it is *learned* by the child from watching the actions and reactions of those around him in childhood.

As Bruner writes in 'the act of interacting' between people, we 'create the world into which the child enters.'

We create their culture and their values.

Chapter 34

How Language Influences The Way We See The World

Not only *how* mother tongue is used can create the child's view of the world, as in the story of Mary and Michael above, but also *which* language is spoken can affect the way we see the world.

To illustrate what I mean here I will give you a few examples.

In English, the tide goes 'in and out'. Literally translated the equivalent French phrase, (if you translate word for word), has the tide going 'up and down.' Both are obviously correct interpretations of the reality of tidal movements, but each emphasises a different aspect of this.

In English 'the past is behind us and the future is before us'. But again, if you translate word for word from the Greek equivalent, 'the past is before us and the future is behind us.' The logic here is that the past faces us because we have lived through it and know what has happened, whereas the future cannot be seen as yet, and so it is behind us.

From Hindi the phrase, ' kal, aaj aur kal' translates into English as 'yesterday, today and to morrow'. The English language version reflects a linear concept of time; whereas the Hindi by making 'yesterday' and 'to morrow' the *same* word – 'kal' – gives a more cyclical emphasis to a concept of time.

The Welsh word for school is 'ysgol'. The same word means 'ladder'. These are usually two very separate concepts in English speakers thought but to a Welsh speaker the connection of schooling as upward progress is immediate through language. (Baker Foundations of Bilingual Education and Bilingualism,)

In some languages the same one word is used to translate the names of certain colours which are separated out into two words in English. For instance take 'blue' and 'green'. In Welsh these colours are not differentiated by name. The word 'glas' can be used to name the colour of the sea and also the colour of grass. Similar Kurdish and Pashto speakers also have one word only – 'sheen' – to describe a 'blue' sky or a 'green' leaf.

Vietnamese can be even more confusing; the word for 'green' – 'xanh' – can also translate as 'blue' or even 'yellow'.

In such a manner the individual human perception of fairly objective reality – tides, time, schooling, colours – is guided by the mother tongue we speak.

In some languages, like Japanese in particular, this interconnection of language and thought is given further expression by the existence of different formulas of speech which will be normally used for addressing others, one style for superiors, another for inferiors.

This is similar to what is called '*takaluf*' in Urdu. Words which would translate as the same word in English are in fact different in Urdu; and are used to reflect the speaker's perception of the rank of the listener.

For instance, the Urdu 'tu', 'tum' and 'aap' are all forms of the pronoun 'you' in English.

'Tu' is used for a servant or perceived inferior, 'tum' for a child, while 'aap' is reserved for elders, or is used in any instance where the speaker wishes to show respect for the listener.

Similarly verb endings change with perceived rank. Whereas a child would be told, 'baitho' (sit), or 'ao', (come) an elder would be asked to 'baithie', or 'ayyie'.

In this manner, the *actual words* used in everyday speech, indoctrinate the learner into the manners and customs of the society he lives in.

Even the child's ability to grasp fairly abstract concepts, like maths, can be affected by mother tongue.

Take a look at this table which shows the vocabulary used for counting in English compared to that used in Japanese. You will soon see two factors here which give the Japanese speaking child an advantage over an English speaking child when it comes to learning to count.

First there are *twenty seven different words* in English needed to count up to ninety nine. These are one, two, three, four, five, six, seven, eight,

How Language Influences The Way We See The World

nine, ten, eleven, twelve, thirteen, fourteen, fifteen, sixteen, seventeen, eighteen, nineteen, twenty, thirty, forty, fifty, sixty, seventy, eighty, ninety.

The Japanese need *only ten words* to do the same.

One	*ichi*
Two	*ni*
Three	*san*
Four	*shi*
Five	*go*
Six	*roku*
Seven	*shichi*
Eight	*hachi*
Nine	*kyu*
Ten	*ju*

(You will also note that the *very sounds* of these words are all very close to the sounds an infant can say early in his speaking life. The English words are not.)

After ten you combine these words to count up to ninety nine.

Eleven	*ju ichi*	(ten one)
Twelve	*ju ni*	(ten two)
Thirteen	*ju san*	(ten three)
Fourteen	*ju shi*	(ten four)
Fifteen	*ju go*	(ten five)
Sixteen	*ju roku*	(ten six)
Seventeen	*ju shichi*	(ten seven)
Eighteen	*ju hachi*	(ten eight)
Nineteen	*ju kyu*	(ten nine)
Twenty	ni ju	(two tens)
Twenty one	ni ju ichi	(two tens and one)

And so on all the way up to ninety nine.

Then you need '*Hyaku*' for a hundred. So for example 150 would be *hyaku go ju*.

Apart from less vocabulary needed to express number than in English, the actual *language structure* of the counting system leads the child to a quicker understanding of place value.

So for 'twenty' the Japanese child will learn 'two ten'. Some poor teacher further along the line will find it much easier to explain that the 2 in 20 is two tens, and so on. Instead of rows of sums set out under the headings H (hundreds) T (tens) and U (units) as English speaking children do to help get them to grasp the significance of place value, the Japanese child will have absorbed the same information far more quickly and easily through language itself.

Equally a lot of arithmetic is simplified by this system.

Look at say:

11+ 12 = 23.

'Ten one' plus 'ten two' equals ten three.'

Eleven plus twelve equals twenty three would be the English reading of that.

I'm sure you can invent many more examples for your self, and see the many ways this naming system facilitates mathematical understanding.

So the issue now arises, 'How much does the mother tongue we speak affect the way we see the world?'

Some researchers conclude it has a huge effect, others are not so convinced.

Of those who claim that our thoughts are under the control of our language the two most famous are Sapir and Whorf. According to them, their research work in language leads to the conclusion that the way we view the world is—

'along the lines laid down by our native languages. The categories and types that we isolate from the world of phenomena we do not find there because they stare every observer in the face.'

So for instance an English speaker 'sees' the tides going in and out; whereas a French speaker 'sees' them going up and down.

The way they perceive the world is controlled by the very structure of the language they speak.

The Sapir-Whorf hypothesis continues,

'We cut nature up, organise it into concepts, and ascribe significances as we do, largely because we are parties to an agreement that holds throughout our speech community and is codified in the patterns of our language.'

Certainly they have drawn attention to the possible effects of different languages on perception. And of course we are all, to some extent, unconsciously influenced by the language we speak.

However we are capable of thought and can readily accommodate another viewpoint if it is described and explained to us in mother tongue. Using only English here we can see the French language viewpoint! Besides English speakers have observed the same tidal phenomena as the French, since they use phrases like, 'high' tide and 'low' tide!

At any rate, very few people nowadays are confined to one language only. The learning of a second language is almost obligatory in contemporary secondary schools.

How does competence in more than one language affect thinking?

Well, look at the example I gave above of a French speaker seeing tides going up and down. The English speaker sees the same tides going in and out.

So it seems only reasonable to conclude then that a bilingual speaker of both languages would have a clearer picture of tidal movements than a monolingual who spoke only one of these languages. The bilingual would know that the tides perform *both* types of movements 'up and down' *and* 'in and out'.

The bilingual is – of necessity – forced to think more carefully than a monolingual. The resulting intellectual or cognitive benefits of bilingualism are well documented.

Chapter 35

The Benefits Of Bilingualism

There is now overwhelming and conclusive evidence for the cognitive benefits of bilingualism. Put briefly, here are some of them.

Long before a baby utters his first word he has to sort out the particular sounds and structures of the sentences he hears around him. He is learning to classify!

The bilingual has to go through a further sorting and classifying process to gain his second language.

He not only has to store two words for the one object, he also must remember when to use which language. If the child is an early bilingual, this ability to sort, distinguish and classify will aid in the later development of maths and reading skills.

Increased creativity, especially in story telling, is another gain. Baker (Foundation of Bilingual Education and Bilingualism) suggests that this might be because he is 'less bound by words, more elastic in thinking.'

Through language he can see more than one viewpoint and so have more options for his story.

Bilinguals are also ahead on an awareness of how a language is used. Now all young children have the ability to think about language itself, but in the bilingual this ability is inevitably much more highly developed.

From about three years of age onwards Erin asked many questions about what things she had heard *meant*.

There are numerous examples from children showing this ability to think about words.

Now obviously for a bilingual this process is increased quite dramatically. Not only must they question correct procedure in *two* languages but also they must cope with sometimes opposing viewpoints expressed through language itself; such as the tides in French and English which I have described earlier. Here they have to consider the 'in and out' and also the 'up and down.'

They are yet not finished. They then have to work out their own view of this apparent conflict. They have to evolve a *third* way of looking which encompasses both points of view!

This must involve a great deal of exercise for the young brain!

To get a better idea of the thinking processes involved in this, here is a sample test used originally by Piaget to test children's control of language and meaning.

Suppose all speakers of English agreed that from this moment on, everyone would call the sun the moon, and the moon the sun.

What would be in the sky at night when we go to bed? (Answer: the sun.)

Would the sky be bright or dark? (Answer: dark.)

How the child pays attention to language is controlled in this task. The child has to focus attention on the new meanings and not be misled by former ones. Both fully bilingual and partially bilingual children significantly outscored monolinguals in their responses to the sun/moon problem (Bialystok 1991).

As Laura Ann Petitto, researcher in children's language working in New Orleans says,

'Being bilingual can give you a cognitive edge.'

If you look on the internet you will find that convincing evidence for the cognitive flexibility of bilingual children is now fully recognised. There has also been research into research into the cognitive skills of elderly bilinguals. It has been proven that the cognitive skills of the elderly bilingual do not slow down in old age as rapidly as the same skills in monolinguals.

I think that the key to understanding this beneficial effect is explained very clearly by Bialystok and Kenji Hakuta in their book 'In Other Words':-

....'knowing two languages is much more than simply knowing two ways of speaking'...

(the bilingual)... 'has entertained possibilities that the monolingual speaker has had no need to entertain...'

Remember the samples I gave of literal translation from one language to another?

They continue...

'it is precisely because the structures and concepts of different languages never coincide that the experience of learning a second language is so spectacular in its effects.'

One is *forced* to think!

Apart from the cognitive benefits, there are very definite and obvious social and economic benefits to becoming fluent in another language. There are very good reasons why parents, once they see their child fluent in mother tongue, start to think about helping the child to acquire a second language.

Fortunately, for historical reasons mainly, there is very detailed research into the best way to do this. It is now clear what forms the best way to teach and learn a second language.

Much of this research into bilingualism was a practical response to the effects of the vast movements of population in recent world history. Initially the United States was the recipient of millions of European migrants, many of whom spoke little or no English. Then the last fifty or sixty years saw the start of really significant migrations of people to England. A lot of this migration continues to the present day.

Many are facilitated by late 20th century improvements in air travel; and are triggered by wars, natural disasters, political decisions, or economic necessity. These migrants speak their home language, and arriving in a different language community have to become proficient in a second language if they wish to make a success of their new lives.

Schools in recipient areas especially cities, became a microcosm of this changing world. In London schools, where I taught in the 70s, 80s and 90s language surveys we did within school reflected events in the wider world.

Pupils' home languages gave a real clue to recent world history. The Cyprus split into Greek and Turkish areas ensured we had speakers of both languages in our classrooms. The Iran/Iraq war brought Persian and Iraqi speakers.

Plenty of Hindi speakers as a result of Idi Amin's policies in Uganda. Pakistani internal politics led to Urdu, and Punjabi speakers.

Troubles in Sudan ensured Arabic and Swahili languages listed in our results.

The return of Hong Kong to rule by mainland China led to an increase in Chinese speakers.

The Benefits Of Bilingualism

I remember one survey revealed that in a school of roughly 1,000 pupils, we had speakers of 46 languages other than English in our classrooms!

The major recipient countries of these migrations in the English speaking world, such as the United States, Great Britain, Australia and New Zealand, found the presence of such pupils a spur to developing learning and teaching styles which with both monolingual and bilingual children in the classroom, would be effective.

This was the case where I was teaching.

I had a personal interest in bilingualism and learning. Partly I should think because of my own education as a child. I am Irish and my father's business interests meant that I often changed schools as a young child. We spoke English at home but some of the schools at that time, the 1940s, [Southern Ireland was declared a Republic in 1949] taught 'through the medium' as it was known. That meant many lessons were in Gaelic. I clearly remember cutting spoken and written answers to the bone because I didn't have the Gaelic words in my head to express my English language thoughts.

Later in London this experience was to prove useful. I had myself experienced what if felt like to be 'dumb' as far as my teachers were aware!

Secondary school for me was more settled, and teaching was mainly through English, which allowed me to fill in various gaps in my understanding of curriculum. Apart from Gaelic lessons themselves, of course, the only subject where the teacher used that language was my Latin teacher! Can you imagine trying to learn a third language through a second language? Multiple early opportunities to understand how it feels to be a language stranger in an unknown land!

Chapter 36

Stephen Krashen

The outstanding name in the world of teaching a second language at the present time is that of American professor, Stephen Krashen. He is a highly acclaimed linguist, initially specialising in theories of language acquisition and development.

More recently, his research has focused on reading, and the effects of reading on both language acquisition and academic success. The book which has brought him most fame is Principles and Practice in Second Language Acquisition. (English Language Teaching series. London: Prentice-Hall International (UK) Ltd.)

His widely accepted theory on second language teaching is recognised as valid and pragmatic by most researchers in this field. Certainly I found his thoughts and ideas extremely useful in my own teaching of children speaking a language other than English. Besides everything in my own experience of learning other languages coincided precisely with every word he has written.

The parallels between learning mother tongue and a second language are highly significant and jump off the pages of his writing.

The first key point to note about his work is that he does not write of 'teaching' or 'learning' a second language. He writes about 'language acquisition'; of the student 'acquiring' and not 'learning', a second language.

This extraordinarily corresponds with how an infant learns mother tongue. No formal teaching as such ever takes place. He points out that for adults there are two ways to become competent in a second language.

They can *learn* it or else they can *acquire* it.

Language learning is really learning 'about' a language, its rules, grammar, way of naming things and so on.

Language acquisition on the other hand is not a conscious process. It is 'getting a message through' while engaged in other activities. It is a subconscious process. "In non-technical language, acquisition is 'picking-up' a language."

This is a brief description of Krashen's widely known and well accepted theory of second language acquisition, which has had a great impact in all areas of second language research and teaching since the 1980s.

Take a look at the following essential elements of his theory. In italics I will remind you of a child learning mother tongue.

"......thousands of people have acquired second languages throughout history, and in many cases acquired them very well. They acquired second languages while they were focused on something else, while they were gaining interesting or needed information, or interacting with people they liked to be with."

Baby is concentrated on getting his needs satisfied, he is playing with his minders.

"...error correction has little affect on language acquisition."

Remember the 'fis' phenomenon?

"In the real world, conversations with sympathetic native speakers who are willing to help the acquirer understand are very helpful."

Parents and caretakers seem, almost intuitively, to understand this need for a willingness to help a child understand. They will describe, repeat, explain and demonstrate in an effort to convey meaning.

"What theory implies, quite simply, is that language acquisition, first or second, occurs when comprehension of real messages occurs".....

'Do you want a bottle? Here's your bottle!' a real message of immediate interest to the child.

and when the acquirer is not 'on the defensive'...

'Who's a clever little baby then?'

Language acquisition does not require extensive use of conscious grammatical rules, and does not require tedious drill.

'No baby! Repeat after me: I am, he is, she is, you are, we are' etc. Have you ever heard this?

It does not occur overnight, however. Real language acquisition develops slowly, and speaking skills emerge significantly later than listening skills, even when conditions are perfect.

Baby shows understanding long before he talks.

The best methods are therefore those that supply 'comprehensible input' in low anxiety situations, containing messages that students really want to hear.

'Hello baby! Are you awake then? Mummy's here!'

These methods do not force early production in the second language, but allow students to produce when they are 'ready', recognizing that improvement comes from supplying communicative and comprehensible input, and not from forcing and correcting production.

Have you ever heard,'No baby! Don't say 'mama!' The correct word is 'Mother'!

The optimum way for a student to acquire language is when he is be exposed to 'comprehensible input' which is roughly tuned to a level slightly higher than he can himself produce. He should listen to language pitched at a *slightly* higher level than his own current productive ability. As Krashen puts it, 'Production ability emerges. It is not taught directly.' Because the new vocabulary is embedded in a familiar context the learner can acquire its meaning.

Just as the child learning mother tongue understands meaning because all of the talk directed to him is about the 'here and now' so there are enough clues for the second language learner to work out new words which are part of the current communication. Caretaker speech is so effective in teaching the child that it is obvious that teacher talk should follow a similar pattern.

This is called 'instructional scaffolding'.

'Mummy car.'

'Yes. That is mummy's car'.

Instructional scaffolding has been described as the help and support offered to a learner when he is faced with acquiring a new concept or skill. These supports are slowly removed as the learner gains proficiency himself in the task.

So we have come full circle and are back with the toddler and his building bricks! Back to Vygotsky's Zone of Proximal Development!

Finally, Krashen observes that a number of 'affective variables' play a facilitating role in second language acquisition. He refers to what he calls the 'Affective Filter'. This affective or emotional state filter determines whether acquisition will take place or not.

New learning has to reach the brain so to speak, through this 'filter'.

The filter performs a role rather like the portcullis entrance in ancient castles. When it is lifted up the gateway is unobstructed, and people can move freely through it. When it is down the entrance is blocked and no movement can take place. It acts as a filter to the castle. In a similar fashion, the state of mind of the learner will determine whether new information will access the brain or not.

Depending on whether it is 'up' or down' it will either aid or prevent acquisition of new input.

He has shown that those best equipped for learning have:-
1. High motivation.
2. Self-confidence.
3. A good self-image.
4. A low level of anxiety.

The filter is up, and therefore not blocking new knowledge from entering the brain. The pathways are open to new input.

However, equally, the affective filter can be down and so form a 'mental block.' The doorway is then shut to acquisition.

This happens to the learner with:-
1. Low motivation.
2. Low self-esteem.
3. Debilitating anxiety.

If you look back once again at this final section you will realise instantly that the Affective Filter as described by Krashen does not apply only to learning a second language.

It applies to ALL learning!

Think about something you have learned since leaving school. Take learning to drive a car for instance. Remember how you felt about the process to begin with. Did your attitude affect your progress?

I think it is obvious that if we want to do something, and are confident that we can, then success is inevitable. Equally if we believe we will fail then failure is what we will get.

Chapter 37
_____

Between Two Languages

Some people are reluctant for a child to learn a second language because they feel that this may take away from the child's ability to speak mother tongue. This is in much the same way that some parents have expressed concern about teaching Baby Sign. They think it may slow up actual speech production.

There is much testimony to the fact that this is not true. Indeed the very opposite effect is reported over and over again. There are still many misconceptions about the effects of second language learning on a child's development.

I would like more people, both parents and teachers, to be aware of some of the issues involved. For instance, when Erin started at nursery school I noticed that there were quite a handful of children in her class who did not speak English. Through chat with other mothers, my daughter Sarah came across the story one of these children, Max. He was a three year old child with Cantonese speaking parents, and so obviously his home language was Cantonese. His mother, Lucy, told Sarah that because he was having difficulty settling at school she needed help with his English. She felt that the language barrier, allied to a child's very natural distrust of a new and strange environment, were proving too much for him.

Lucy came to the U.K. from Hong Kong in the mid 90s. She was then 14. Her parents placed her in a secondary school, where they were assured of special language facilities for speakers of other languages. In actual fact, this turned out to be Lucy being removed from mainstream lessons and brought to another room. Here she was shown books and videos, and basically told to work out her own course of study and get on with it! So justifiably, in the light of her own experience, she had little faith that Max would fare any better than she had done herself.

Lucy was very excited to hear that I had been a teacher. She immediately saw me as a potential solution to her problem in that she saw me as a teacher of English who would support her efforts to teach Max the language.

I found it hard to tell her that the best thing she could do for Max was to continue to speak Cantonese at home, to read to him in Cantonese, and so build up his knowledge and understanding of the world through home language.

Then when he was in school he would already have *knowledge* about the world around him and would only need the new *names* for ideas and concepts he already understood.

She had thought, as most people in a similar position do, that she should struggle with English at home. But her grasp of the language was not strong enough, and I had seen too many children in my time, from a variety of backgrounds, virtually 'fall between two languages.'

Plus, equally importantly, Max would lose his ability to speak Cantonese as fluently and easily as he could otherwise have done.

He reminded me of a little girl I met years ago in London. This 11 year old whom I shall call Maria, was just starting secondary school. She had a bright and bubbly personality, seemed to have a natural intelligence, and was interested in everything. But something about her use of language and approach to life made her seem like a much younger child, or a like a bilingual speaking a second language. Curious, I looked up her admission notes. A completely English speaking background.

Odd.

Then two weeks later I met her parents at a school function. When they spoke their English was quite heavily accented, and frequently grammatically incorrect. As we chatted they relaxed and told me more of Maria's background.

They could not have children of their own and so they had adopted Maria when she was three. At that time she was living in Cyprus, speaking Greek, and came from a purely Greek cultural background.

The adoptive parents were from a similar background, but they decided, that as they were already in England, and as she was going to live in England with them, that they would not speak Greek to her in her new life. They would try not to use the language when she was within earshot.

So when she came to England they made a huge effort and used only English speaking to the child.

This did explain her performance in the language.

I will leave it to you to imagine what it must have felt like to be three year old Maria....

However she was blessed with her adoptive parents who must have been marvellous to her to have produced such a confident and outgoing child. With understanding of her language needs, the school was able to supply the support she needed to catch up on her peers, and in fact to do extremely well in later years.

Another child was not so fortunate. Ayse was 14 when I first met her. She was a lovely, calm, dreamy sort of person, who smiled at everyone but never herself contributed to class work. Her written work was minimalist to put it kindly. She could spend half an hour writing a heading for work and underlining it.

It was devastating to me the day I realised that she had, at best, an eight or nine year old's comprehension of English language, the language of the school.

I went around after school to meet her parents. They ran a shop in the local High street. They were lovely caring people. Their home language was Turkish, but of course for Andrea's sake they spoke only their fractured grasp of English when she was within hearing distance. So she spoke no Turkish. The poor girl had only the smallest amount of either language with which to express her thoughts.

So parents of children who speak a different language at home to that of the school do need advice and guidance from those responsible for educating the child. If a child is fluent in *any* mother tongue then the work of the school is lessened. This should be made clear to parents as soon as the child starts in the education system. No one at the nursery had spoken to Lucy about these issues. Since this was so, it seems logical to conclude that equally the parents of the other non English speaking pupils in the class had not been given any help or advice.

This is really aggravating when it is the *minimum* one would expect a receiving teacher to do for such parents.

Consider what schools do when they provide a quality education. They provide a child with **knowledge and literacy.**

Take knowledge.

If a child already understands how things work in his home language then he doesn't need to learn this knowledge again. He already knows it. All he has to do now is learn the new *names* for the words he already uses at home. Working in school the knowledge of things he has acquired through first language make what he hears or reads in school easier to understand.

Now consider literacy.

If the child can already read in mother tongue then this is even better again. This is because reading skills learned in the first language transfer to the second language. Very obviously it is easier for a child to learn to read in a language he understands.(Smith 1994) Reading is making sense of symbols on a page. Once reading skill is present in any one language a child understands reading in general.

Chapter 38

Methods of Measuring Language Ability

What level of language has a child?
More and more schools are recognising that language itself can be a barrier to a child's learning. The question is how do you assess the language level of those you are teaching?
There is detailed guidance available to schools if they care to use it.
For example, the Home Office issued the following guidelines to help evaluate at what stage of learning each new bilingual speaker would be. They are very straightforward and easy to use.
Initially this guidance was made available to teachers to assess the level of English in children who spoke a different language at home.
But what is obvious, if you stop and think for a second or two, is that it could be equally useful in assessing the level of *any* child in a classroom, **even if the home language is English.**

The four stages of progress are:-

Stage One – new to English – Beginner
Stage Two – becoming familiar with English – Elementary
Stage Three – becoming confident as a user of English – Intermediate
Stage Four – a very fluent user of English in most social and learning contexts – Advanced

METHODS OF MEASURING LANGUAGE ABILITY

Stage One – new to English

Makes contact with another child in the class. Joins in activities with other children, but may not speak. Uses non-verbal gestures to indicate meaning – particularly needs, likes and dislikes. Watches carefully what other children are doing, and often imitates them. Listens carefully and often "echoes" words and phrases of other children and adults. Needs opportunities for listening to sounds, rhythms and tunes of English through songs, rhymes, stories and conversations. If young may join in repetitive chorus of a story. Beginning to label objects in the classroom, and personal things. Beginning to put words together in holistic phrases (e.g. me no want, not go, etc.). May be involved in classroom learning activities in the first language with children who speak the same first language. May choose to use first language only in most contexts. May be willing to write in the first language (if he or she can), and if invited to. May be reticent with unknown adults. May be very aware of negative attitudes by peer group to the first language. May choose to move into English through story and reading, rather than speaking.

Stage Two – becoming familiar with English

Growing confidence in using the English s/he is acquiring. Growing ability to move between languages, and to hold conversations with peer groups. Simple holistic phrases may be combined or expanded to create new ideas. Beginning to sort out small details (e.g. "he" and "she" distinction) but more interested in communicating meaning than in "correctness". Increasing control of the English tense system in particular contexts, such as story-telling, reporting events and activities that s/he has been involved in, and from book language. Understands more English that s/he can use. Growing vocabulary for naming objects and events, and beginning to qualify nouns with adjectives (e.g. colour, size, quantity) and using simple adverbs. Increasingly confident in taking part in activities with other children through English. Beginning to write simple stories, often modeled on those s/he has heard read aloud. Beginning to write simple accounts of activities s/he has been involved in, but may need considerable support. Confident enough to substitute words from his/her first language if s/he needs to. Continuing to rely on support of his/her friends. Very sensitive to criticism of peers about his/her use of the first and second language.

Stage Three – becoming confident as a user of English

Shows great confidence in using English in most social situations. This confidence may mask the need for support in taking on other registers (e.g. science investigation, historical research). Growing command of the syntactic structure, and developing an understanding of metaphor and pun. Widening vocabulary from reading of story, poems and information books and from being involved in maths and science investigations, and other curriculum areas. May choose to explore complex ideas (such as drama/role play) in the first language with children who share the same first language. Increasingly sure of development of the verb system (e.g. relationships of time, use of modal verbs), the pronoun system, and sentence structure. Pronunciation may be very native-speaker like, especially that of young children.

Stage Four – a very fluent user of English in most social and learning contexts

A very experienced user of English, and exceptionally fluent in many contexts. May continue to need support in understanding subtle nuances of metaphor, and in anglo-centric cultural content in poems and literature. Confident in exchanges and collaboration with English-speaking peers. Writing confidently in English with a growing competence over different genre. Continuing new development in English often related to writing. Will move with ease between English and the first language depending on the contexts s/he is in, what s/he judges appropriate, and the encouragement of the school.

This simple categorising is obviously very helpful to staff in helping describe the level of language comprehension of those bilinguals they are teaching.

I would suggest that the two latter stages are just as useful to assess the language level of a <u>monolingual</u>, especially in secondary education.

Further research by Dr. Jim Cummins of the University of Toronto led to the refining of this outline when he introduced the idea of BICS and CALP to define the language ability of a bilingual student.
BICS is an acronym for Basic Interpersonal Communicative Skills, CALP for Cognitive Academic Language Proficiency.

The names are almost self evident descriptions of the levels they describe.

BICS is the ordinary day by day speech of a native language speaker in everyday normal situations.

CALP on the other hand, as the name suggests, is the language style of those who have been exposed to, and learned from, academic or formal educational input.

Research by Cummins showed that for a bilingual to achieve BICS can take from one and a half to two years. However to achieve CALP comparable to that of a native speaker can take up to five years.

So to achieve CALP is much harder than to achieve BICS.

The next chapter describes in detail each of these levels of language competence.

Chapter 39

BICS and CALP

Basic Interpersonal Communication Skills – BICS

This is the language of being a socially interactive creature. It is the normal everyday talk which occurs between people as they go about their daily business. It is personal and uses words like 'you' and 'I'.

It uses simple straightforward vocabulary, which research in this field has shown to be words mainly of Anglo Saxon or Old English origin. (David Corson).

These words are frequently monosyllabic.

Apart from actual vocabulary BICS uses a host of other 'props' to facilitate understanding. These include gestures, body language, facial expressions, tone of voice and so on.

It allows 'mms' and nods of agreement as well as head shakes of disagreement to ensure meaning between speakers. It allows slang words like 'O.K.', 'yeah' and so on.

A lot of our waking time is spent listening, trying to make sense of the world around us. Few of us speak in full, grammatically correct sentences. Instead there is that familiar shorthand which includes grunts, murmurs, and a continual assault on linguistic rules!

Repetition occurs and a speaker may interrupt himself, or be interrupted to clarify meaning.

If, despite all these clues, a misunderstanding does happen then the speaker is soon made aware of it. This is either because his listener looks totally blank, or else gives a response which indicates that he has either misheard or not understood the message of the speaker.

BICS also uses words of social politeness, like 'please', 'thanks', 'sorry'. In addition, the speaker adjusts his pace of delivery, and choice of wording to his perceived notion of the language level, maturity and intelligence level of his listener.

His speech is appropriate to each and every nuance of the current situation; this includes the social, intellectual, and relative power positions of speaker and listener, and the context and purpose of the dialogue.

Emotion is not only permissible it is often an integral part of mutual understanding. This is conveyed by emphasis and tone of voice. Indeed the same utterance can have totally different meanings when the tone of voice is varied. *How* you speak can be as informative as what words you use.

What would probably make BICS 100% clear to someone new to the concept is to point out that it is almost exclusively the language used in soaps and popular television dramas. If some character in a show does speak in a CALP way then he is either an Inspector Morse, or is likely to be accused by another character of 'swallowing a dictionary'!

Cognitive Academic Language Proficiency – CALP

CALP is the traditional language of learning, academics and scholars.

As Krashen would probably put it, BICS is 'acquired', whereas CALP is 'learned'. BICS is informal, CALP formal.

While BICS deals with the concrete observable 'here and now'; CALP deals with the abstract.

CALP is the using of language itself as a conscious tool for learning.

Academic texts have usually been carefully edited, and may employ quite complex grammatical structures – clauses, and dependent clauses, for example. This is undoubtedly to avoid error and ensure that information is transmitted in a completely accurate and unambiguous way.

Unlike BICS, there is little interaction, feedback or personal involvement – if any – for the receiver of the information.

The problem is that the grammar structures and vocabulary required to do this are often beyond the comprehension level of the struggling bilingual speaker. Partly this is because 'academic language' differs enormously from 'social language.'

David Corson demonstrated in his findings that up to 60% of the words met with in academic texts are low frequency and have their original roots in Latin or Greek. They are often polysyllabic.

This is in direct contrast to BICS, with its greater level of high frequency, largely monosyllabic words rooted more in Anglo Saxon and Old English.

So the result for the bilingual is failure to access the full curriculum. That is unless teachers and lecturers make informed efforts to overcome this language barrier to academic success.

The division of language into BICS and CALP has met with criticisms. Some objectors – like Spolsky 1984 – disapprove of the actual acronyms themselves. This is because the names in themselves give added value to CALP over BICS.

Thus, while 'communication skills' might be the equivalent of 'language proficiency'; 'basic' is certainly of lesser value than 'cognitive academic'. So the result is that CALP is viewed as a superior means of communication.

This is a clever observation, but it does not detract from the validity of the fact that their use draws attention to the truth of the matter that *two very different styles of language are used in formal and informal learning situations.*

Besides, CALP *is* superior in advanced learning situations where precision in language is required to *accurately* express thought. Equally it is inferior to BICS as an everyday means of communicating with others!

Similarly further objections pointed out that school is not the only place where higher cognitive skills are required. *Academic intelligence* and *social intelligence* can make equally complex demands on a person. (Genesee 1984)

The socially skilled speaker must be sensitive to the appropriateness of wording, and every tiny nuance of meaning in different social situations. They must be prepared to operate effectively, even in unfamiliar circumstances.

The objections are both clever observations, but neither detracts from the validity of the fact that their use draws attention to the truth of the matter that **two very different styles of language are used in formal and informal learning situations.**

So despite these objections, BICS and CALP are a very useful shorthand to describe two different sets of competence in a bilingual's language control. They draw the educator's attention to the essential role of *language* itself – as opposed to subject specific *content* – in the study of any subject.

Cummins writes...

'Some heretofore neglected aspects of language proficiency are considerably more relevant for students' cognitive and academic progress than are the surface manifestations of proficiency frequently focused on by education'

and he goes on to add that....

'educators' failure to appreciate these differences can have particularly unfortunate consequences for language minority students.' (1992, p. 17)

You will realise how right he is by remembering the story of Ayse above.

She was one pupil who slipped through the education net, when none of her teachers managed to see how basic her language skills were.

Chapter 40

BICS and CALP in a Monolingual Classroom

This is research and its results all conducted with bilingual pupils in mind.

However in the light of my own teaching experience I would say that this idea of using BICS and CALP in the classroom has enormous implications for every learner – **whether or not he is bilingual.**

Pupils who speak English at home are in a sense being placed in a position of learning a second language when they start school, even though the school apparently speaks the same language as the home. Every subject they study has its own terminology, and use of this subject specific vocabulary starts for the child at quite a young age.

They come to school with BICS, but find very rapidly that teachers 'speak another language.'

Teachers use CALP.

For any child to settle in and do well at school he needs to have two sets of linguistic ability. Firstly they need to be able to communicate with others face to face (BICS). But to succeed academically they have to learn to use a second, more formal method of communication (CALP).

Here are two real examples to illustrate what I mean.

When my eldest son was thirteen he had his first chemistry lesson. After only one lesson he was already fascinated with the subject and determined to learn all he could. He said his homework was easy and that he knew exactly what he had to do.

BICS and CALP in a Monolingual Classroom

A few days later he came in from school feeling quite down. 'I don't know what I left out or what happened Mum, but I only got two out of ten for that chemistry homework!'

Sure enough at the bottom of his work the teacher had written 2/10, and nothing else! He had no clue as to where he had gone wrong.

I looked at his work and instantly saw the reason for the low mark.

Instead of putting headings like 'Aim', 'Equipment needed', 'Method', 'Results' and 'Conclusion' and writing in the passive voice style of such exercises (the Bunsen burner was placed…..) he had written a chatty style account of the lesson.

'When we went into the classroom we were told …'

Once he understood the format required, he always got high grades for his work.

The second incident is not so straightforward though memorable nevertheless. My youngest child was 14 when I received a phone call from his headmaster to see him urgently on a disciplinary matter. In the meantime he was excluding my son from all history lessons.

What on earth had he done?

Apparently the class had a lesson on Emily Pankhurst and the suffragette movement. For homework they were each handed an account of one suffragette. She had organised a meeting for women, hired a hall, organised and printed leaflets, and engaged a band as an additional attraction for the event. On the planned date no one turned up. The homework was to describe how she felt when no one attended her meeting. I was shown his work.

The question was written out as a heading, and underlined. The date was neatly written.

So far so good.

Then his answer.

This answer which led to exclusion, and needed all my earnest promises of excellent behaviour on my son's part in future in order to end the matter, was…

'Gutted.'

Later when I said to him that he was supposed to describe how hard it was in those days to stand out for women's rights, and how much work this woman had done to further the cause, he replied, 'But Mum, the teacher *knows* all that! She told *us*!'

He was probably being rather 'tongue in cheek' but nevertheless there is a real need to tell pupils exactly what a teacher expects in an adequate answer. And that using a straightforward BICS style answer – while it may be perfectly understood and acceptable in everyday conversation – can lead not only to no mark, but also a reputation for being unacceptably impudent!

I have taken some examples of CALP from two books, one Maths, one English, designed for 10 to 11 year olds, in final year Primary School. These are taken from books covering material in Key Stage 2 of the National Curriculum.

So we have not even reached secondary level as yet.

Maths
Calculate, difference, multiplication, divisor, graph, decimal, fraction, denominator, co-ordinates, polygon, angle, triangle, degrees, rhombus, prime number, factors, multiple, square number, triangular number, average, area, volume, percentage, approximation, probability.

This is no way a complete list of the words a child will meet with in Maths lessons before transfer to secondary school at the age of 11. I think you will agree that these words are not those generally found in everyday communication in the home, or in the school playground.

This language issue in maths can start at quite a young age. At 5.8 Erin could do simple addition and subtraction with numbers under 20. She probably didn't know that what she was doing was actually called 'addition' or 'subtraction'. She knew that five add four is nine, or ten take away two is eight.

One evening she asked for help with the maths work sheet she had for homework.

'I've read it but I can't do this kind of maths!'

We took a look. The work sheet asked some apparently very simple questions.

Subtract two from ten.

What number is five more than four?

And so on.

Suddenly the simple maths was beyond her, obscured by the wording of the questions.

This reminded me of a homework club that I held after school when I was concerned that bilingual pupils might fail through not understanding what was required of them to do for their homework. Initially designed for bilinguals, myself and the other teacher involved in running it were somewhat surprised to find our service was of **equal value** to English speaking monolinguals.

Our rules were simple. You came to the club not to *do* your homework but to find out exactly *how* to do it. Many of the questions involved maths. We both grew very used to people saying, 'Oh! Is that all it means?'

This remark came from nearly every pupil when light was cast on what they had thought was a major piece of work.

So much for the language of maths.

Let's take a look at English lessons themselves and see if things get easier.

English

Index, compound words, prefix, comprehension, character, verb, tense, adverb, suffix, thesaurus, adjectives, synonyms, punctuation, apostrophe, inverted commas, abbreviations, homophone, analogy, negatives, phrase, sentence, conjunction, simile, metaphor, idiom, dictionary, glossary, essay.

They do not get easier at all as you can see and this is really in one sense a double whammy. Before the child goes to school they believe that they can speak English, good enough to get them by in any situation. After some of these lessons they may be more doubtful!

BICS may be the sole language through which a child communicates with a teacher and classmates and thus give the impression of understanding far more of the content of lessons than any one realises. The child uses all manner of (quite clever really!) subterfuges and cunning ploys to disguise his failure to understand really what the teacher is getting at.

Indeed they often employ far more initiative, originality and intelligence in disguising their lack of comprehension than would be required to understand it in the first instance if only the teacher knew this!

This can include writing slowly so that a quicker child near him can let him copy an answer; or perhaps give time for another child to ask the teacher to explain what it is that is needed for the answer.

He may be good at detecting which line of information in his text book contains the answer he needs and copy it out quite mindlessly.

He could indulge in some minor misbehaviour, as it is better from him his point of view to be seen as 'a bit cheeky' rather than stupid.

Or it could be a maths lesson where a teacher has read through one or two worked questions in a text book and now the children are expected to do a number of similar problems on their own. All he has to do here is follow the formula of moves made in the examples and he is home and dry – a veritable mathematician.

The Language Barrier

As one nine year old girl, a friend's daughter, explained to me when I asked her what was it she did she not understand in the maths question she was set for homework. It was to do with some addition of fractions. Her mother had asked me to help her, because of the child's very poor end of term test results.

'Oh! You don't have to *understand* maths to *do* maths'.

She was quite sorry for me and my ignorance, and went on to explain.

'It's quite simple really. In these sums you just do the same as the teacher does and it comes out right. I've just forgotten some of what she does.'

I'm sure you can see here that this child's teacher, instead of trying to ensure that the children *understood* what they were doing and why, had instead given them a 'prescription' to follow mindlessly to ensure exercise books full of 'good' work.

This was certainly so with this little girl. She had two exercise books full of work ticked and marked as 'correct.' So while apparently 'making good progress' the child in fact had only learned to copy formulas, and as a result understood very little of the work in her book.

Chapter 41

A Lesson Where Children Use Language

In my own years of teaching, because there were so many bilingual pupils in each classroom, I obviously had to work at devising lessons which would allow the bilinguals to fully understand what was going on. This involved introducing and implementing a whole range of teaching and learning styles, which would allow *pupils* to focus more on actually *using* the language needed to understand the new information or concepts.

Learning styles refer to people's *preferred* methods of information intake or approaches to learning. The learning styles of younger students change as they age, because their brain is constantly developing.

Learning styles can be divided into three basic categories: auditory, visual, and tactile/kinaesthetic. There are then many sub divisions of these but for now the basics are enough to see that learners need a wide range of teaching styles to match their equally wide range of learning styles.

Tactile/kinaesthetic learners prefer learning through touching or moving. They want a physical or hands-on approach.

Auditory learners prefer learning through listening. They want a teacher to talk them through new information.

Visual learners prefer learning through seeing. They want to read the new information for themselves instead of having their teacher explain it verbally.

We tend to cater for auditory and visual more than tactile/kinaesthetic in schools.

But the good classroom makes provision for all styles of learning. This is especially needed when trying to encourage pupils to actively use new vocabulary. After all the four sequential steps towards developing language fluency are:-

1. Understanding.
2. Speaking.
3. Reading.
4. Writing.

And as I have pointed out earlier, the child must first experience – hands on – the world before he can label it. So if this is the easiest way to access understanding, then if we want school children to develop CALP we must figure out ways to make lesson plans which accommodate this approach. That is, there is a need to include tactile/kinaesthetic learning even in more strictly academic formal classroom situations.

Recently I saw a class of nine or ten year olds who were back from visiting a safari park where conservation of endangered species had been the focus of the visit. So they had had experience of seeing the creatures for themselves. This was good experience to base a future lesson on.

The teacher sat on a chair to the front of the room, while the pupils gathered round sitting on a carpet on the floor, in three lines across in front of her.
Teacher asked the class,
'Which was your favourite animal today at the safari park?'
There was a good show of hands, and teacher indicated one pupil to reply. The child did so.
Teacher asked,
'Was there any other animal anyone else liked ?'
Another show of hands, another child selected to reply.
Teacher asked, 'Are any of these animals endangered species?'
From another show of hands a child is selected to reply.
And so on. You get the picture.

Notice that here **teacher talks far more than the children**. Indeed, some of them never get a chance to say a word. Still this is often a very normal format for a primary school class.

Now suppose the teacher took a different approach.
First she would analyse the new vocabulary terms she wished the children to know by the end of the lesson.
These are probably, *conservation, conservationist, endangered, species, extinct, game warden, game reserve, poacher, poaching, habitat,*

A Lesson Where Children Use Language

natural habitat. After their visit to the safari park they will already know the names of some endangered species. They will have heard some or all of the words in the list above.

One way to ensure every child would have a chance to understand, speak, read and write these new words would be by using the following type of lesson plan.

The children are seated in groups of four facing each other. If you have odd numbers over four it is better to have a group of three, or two groups of five rather than a two. The teacher is no longer confined to the front facing the class but moves down the room where she is almost instantly available to any group who might raise a hand for help.

A 'cloze' passage of writing is one in which key words are omitted from sentences and have to be supplied in spaces left blank for the purpose. The teacher should prepare in advance a cloze passage which will involve using all the new terminology.

An example would be:-

"Here are some of the words you will need to fill in the gaps in the sentences below.

Habitat, game warden, poachers, species, poaching, conservation, extinct, conservationist, endangered species, game reserve.

1. A kind of creature who needs help to survive is called an ....
2. If one kind of animal no longer lives on earth it is said to be ....
3. A place where animals are free and safe to live is called a ....
4. The work of protecting animals is called ....
5. The home of an animal is called its ....
6. People who kill animals for profit are called ....
7. A person who works on a Game Reserve is called a ....
8. A person who works in or helps with conservation is called a ....
9. Killing elephants and stealing their tusks is called ....
10. Each different kind of animal is called a ....

Finally, can you name any endangered species?"

A copy of this work sheet is in each child's place. To begin with the teacher reads through the full sheet for the whole class. She reads slowly and carefully through each key word at the top of the ten sentences giving a little information and examples of each word there. This lesson is not a test. The aim is for every group to get 100% correct answers, without actually dictating the correct words to the children.

The class is told that each group works together as a team to sort out the correct answers. If they cannot agree they can put their hand up for help. If such help is asked for the teacher gives it freely.

Take 'habitat' for instance. The teacher reads 'habitat' and says something along the lines of, 'Every living creature has some kind of habitat, or place where it is happiest to live. So for a human this would be say a house, or a flat, or for a crow maybe it would be a nest high up in a tree. So really a habitat is a home.' And so on.

When all ten sentences are completed and written out by all the groups the teacher goes through each, one by one, and the children correct their work. It gives them great pleasure to tick correct answers as they go. Also they enjoy the responsibility of doing their own corrections.

Another advantage for the teacher here is that she can focus full attention on the words in front of her and not have to make a continual effort to recall all the information she wants the children to absorb. While the teacher is still as firmly as ever in control, the children have more freedom in their work.

And most importantly each child has had the opportunity to understand, speak, read and write the new CALP style vocabulary.

With BICS a child has to learn to 'understand' and 'speak'; for CALP he also needs to 'read' and 'write'. His grasp of BICS *improves* with reading and writing, but I think that it is *essential* to in the process of acquiring CALP.

This is why earlier I put such emphasis on how a parent can help a child at home develop a child's reading and writing skills.

I am convinced that advances in understanding how a bilingual copes in a second language classroom can equally help teachers and educators understand why so often so many *monolingual* pupils fail academically.

Chapter 42

Cracking The CALP Code

As I have said before, teaching in a school where at least half of the pupils spoke a home language other than English it did not take long to dawn on me that various school strategies initially designed to help bilingual pupils were proving of equal value to monolinguals.

Consider the role of BICS and CALP.

Too often I have heard a teacher express surprise at the apparently inexplicable poor exam or test result of a pupil. In other words a self confident and fluent BICS speaker may be seen as making good academic progress despite the fact that a fairly frequent comment on the same learner's school reports is often along the lines of 'a disappointing test result.' The teacher has failed to notice that while the learner is bright and attentive, polite and cooperative in lessons, he is still speaking and thinking in BICS style language and has not grasped CALP.

How to crack the education language code.

Simply an awareness and understanding by the teacher of the role of language in any acquisition of knowledge and skills can on its own work wonders.

If in addition there is a clear understanding of Vygotsky's analysis of how humans assist one another to learn then we are half way there.

However here are some useful pointers.

1. English speaking pupils in English speaking schools benefit as much as bilinguals from a clear focus on the *language* of a subject.

175

The Language Barrier

Here are one or two small examples of subject specific vocabulary.

Ruler (a straight edged measuring stick) in maths is not a ruler (one who governs) in history.

Or *relief* (the height and slope of land) in geography is not the same as *relief* (the lifting of a siege) in history. Just as it is not the *relief* felt by a tired student when the end of the school day arrives!

Neither is relief the initially puzzling interpretation put on this word by a 15 year old (monolingual!) answering a geography question. Asked to describe the relief of a farm – looking at maps and photographs supplied with the question – the following answer was written:

'I have looked very carefully and no Public Conveniences are marked. Perhaps the workers use the lake.'

It is easy to see where so many of the howlers found in school work come from!

2. Do not instantly dismiss wrong answers.

Suppose a child gives a way out answer to a question. From your point of view the answer is wrong. It has neither sense nor meaning. However, pause for a moment to remember that speech is always internally coherent, that is, it makes sense to the speaker. So there is some breakdown in understanding when a child gives an answer different to the one you expected.

Reply with something like, 'That wasn't what I was thinking. Why did you say that?'

The explanations can range from the sublime to the ridiculous. Having taught for years I know. But all have one thing in common. They throw light on a child's interpretation of your lesson, and his thinking. An example of this occurred in a maths lesson I was observing.

The teacher began by quickly sketching three angles on the board. These were a) an obtuse, b) a right, and c) an acute angle. This was obviously a revision of the previous lesson's content.

She asked that everyone write down in their rough book the letter naming the biggest angle.

'Who wrote "a"?'

14 out of 25 hands went up.

'Who wrote "b"?'

The remaining hands went up.

The teacher then used the advice above and asked for a volunteer from those who got 'b' to come up and explain her answer.

Very confidently the girl moved to the board, having picked up a ruler from her desk as she moved.

She used the ruler to demonstrate that the arms on the right angle were longer than those on the obtuse or acute angle and therefore angle 'b' was the biggest. Her classmates who had given the same 'wrong' answer nodded their heads in approval.

The teacher now had clear evidence that nearly half her class had not understood the concept of angle. She also knew where exactly lay their misinterpretation of the meaning of the word. Useful feed back!

3. Before any lesson decide <u>exactly</u> what you expect pupils to know at the end of it. Write this clearly on the board as an opener.

Read it and explain it simply.

You have covered two learning styles – listening and reading – quickly and efficiently! The teacher presumably is aware of the pupil's stage of learning and is here to provide the classroom management and pupil assistance needed to reach today's goal.

(If you have a goal there is always the possibility that you will reach it. If you don't have a goal then the chances of ever reaching it are considerably lessened. If you do have a goal and reach it the result is a feeling of pleasure in achievement.)

You are providing the vocabulary needed to deal with what the pupil is learning here and now. In other words, you are now exactly replicating how the infant learns first language. The more you can promote interactions with and between pupils which involves use of this new vocabulary the more likely it is that positive learning will take place.

4. Be prepared to share the role of teacher in the classroom.

Teaching and learning does not at all require that there is one designated person who has all the answers. Knowledge can actually be *constructed* when people work together in any activity, especially if they are in the process of gaining a particular skill, or understanding new knowledge.

Each individual assists others, and is assisted themselves by others.

Each makes *some* contribution to general understanding.

In doing so each member of the group increases his own potential for future advances.

Learners are empowered when they help one another find correct answers. One or two examples may clarify this attitude in teaching.

The statistically proven success of maths schemes like 'CASE' and 'Lets Think' which encourage collaborative learning in the classroom support this view. In these schemes learners bring their 'common sense' knowledge into the lesson and use it *in discussion with others* to arrive at an understanding of mathematical concepts.

Ask yourself why do bankers, business people, politicians, retailers, councillors – any profession you care to name really – have meetings?

Why do committees have meetings?

Because experience has shown them that working together as a group they can achieve far more *as a group* than any one individual member could achieve on his own.

5. Provide Model answers

If a teacher occasionally provides a model answer to a question, a piece of work or an essay, then the learner will know exactly what he is aiming for.

Another useful lesson using a similar technique is to provide a poor quality answer at the same time. This should not be a piece of work by any student in the group, but rather a piece written by the teacher herself. It should be roughly the same length as the 'good' answer so that size alone is not taken as an indicator of quality. Allow time for the class to work out as many differences as they can between the two, before going through them and indicating in both where marks are lost or gained by the writer.

6. Use Different Teaching Styles.

There is a multiplicity of alternate style lessons available which work very well with small groups of children learning together and which encourage use of CALP. They can be adapted for use in 'games' in the home.

For example, there are many really sound lesson plans, (many described on the internet), which make use for some, if not all, of the time of a lesson using one or other of the following:

Sequencing

Putting photos, words, sentences, or paragraphs in a logical order.

Matching

Putting titles to corresponding pictures, diagrams, sentences, paragraphs.

Role play
In the above lesson this could be as simple as two elephants having a chat about what they would write to a relative they wished to join them in the game reserve.

I have had eleven year olds role play a volcanic explosion! It can be more serious, a character in history explaining the actions they took – whatever. But all encourage talk with a clearly defined purpose, and using the precise vocabulary a teacher would wish a child to grasp fully.

Mixed sentences
Here on one side of the page are the beginnings of sentences, on the other are the endings. The endings are not in correct order and the learner has to draw a line to match the correct pairs to make sense.

Turn the cards
This game is particularly useful for reinforcing mathematical and scientific words. A CALP word is written on one side of a postcard sized card. A definition and example are given on the other side. Cards are placed on the desks word side up.

Children, working in groups, take turns to place a hand on a card and say what should be written on the other side. If they are right they keep the card. If wrong they return it to the table. The teacher may be called on at any time to adjudicate. The child with the most cards at the end is the group 'winner'.

You can then play the 'game' in reverse with the definition on the up side and the child has to give the CALP word to win the card.

These are all techniques which can be adapted to suit any age group from nursery through to sixth form secondary. I know because I have used them with all of these age groups and had the pleasure of seeing youngsters really enjoying learning.

Most important of all is to get pupils to use the language of the new learning themselves. To make educational progress, it is worthless for a student to acquire knowledge without the language needed to express that understanding. On occasion, silence may be golden, but I really believe that *guided*, or *teacher directed*, talk is essential to the learning process.

Chaper 43
───────

Conclusion

The modern infant goes through in his lifetime the same sequence of language learning as developed in Sumeria over centuries. The sheer speed of learning is prodigious, which shows that humans have definitely got better over the years at teaching and learning communication skills! However, there is still a lot more can be done.

It is worth remembering that compulsory education for all has only arrived in the last few centuries in the West. Prior to that education was exclusive to the upper classes and the privileged. This education relied heavily on a knowledge of Latin and classical Greek. Scholars who advanced learning in different fields then tended to use this language to describe their findings.

This explains the preponderance of words in text books with a Latin or classical Greek origin. Since they were both 'dead' languages there was no possibility of the meaning of the words used changing over time. In a living language such as English some words can alter meaning quite rapidly. When I was a child 'gay' meant 'light hearted' or 'bright; in modern English 'gay' has a much different meaning to most people.

Before mass education the everyday functions of language were different for most people. Grammatical correctness was not an issue. More important was survival, and continuing a reasonable existence as a member of a social group. There was minimal movement between different classes, and language served as an obvious boundary to place in society.

This demarcation by language is not unique to the West.

Conclusion

A classical written language developed in China which performed the same function in Chinese society as Latin did in the West. Up to the 20th century all official documents were written in a 2000 years old monosyllabic language. As in the West this language was exclusive to scholars and people of high rank. It wasn't until the cultural revolution of the 20th century that everyday language began to be used in writing. Even now in current day China many newspapers still use classical written language and a person who knows how to write it is given high respect and honour.

Even the prototype language Sumerian eventually performed the same role in society when the region was overrun by the Akkadians.

The Akkadian language replaced Sumerian for all everyday social functions. However the language of religious, royalty and scholars continued for many centuries to be Sumerian.

So there are precedents for language acting as a boundary to power and independence in a society. So it is for many school learners today.

They simply do not understand the language of the school.

The ancient Akkadian rulers, priests and scholars made knowledge exclusive from the vast majority of their people by encoding it in Sumerian. Similarly today much of the key classroom knowledge is encoded in CALP.

Not only can the learner not access the curriculum, but he also finds his current language position reinforced as inferior.

Research with bilingual children shows that where a home language is not positively recognised as being as good as the language of the school as a tool for communication, the speaker tends to reject the language. Not only this, but he also implicitly rejects the values he has learned with the language; and more significantly it is hard for him now to respect those who gave him this language to begin with.

Much the same can happen with monolinguals. When the language of home apparently fails to cope with the language of school what implicit message do you think the student gets? Non standard, though perfectly clearly understood messages, (such as, 'I ain't done nothing wrong Miss!') are given very short shrift.

Just as the bilingual child rejects home language, (and the culture, standards and ideals implicit in it), when the school does not show that it is valued, so the reaction of the monolingual child is no different.

Minimum he is being made clearly aware that his parent's language is not a fully fledged medium of communication. It is no way equal to the language of the school.

If the language isn't equal what kind of people are his parents?

What kind of person is he?

Equally where the home language of a bilingual *is* recognised as having status in his school community his progress is almost assured. He comes to school *knowing* that he does not speak the language of the school so he expects that he must make an effort to learn it. When he does so he reaps all the benefits of the increased cognitive flexibility associated with competent bilingualism. Today, the 'minority' speaker is shown that hitherto ignored languages, such as Cantonese and Urdu, are now being taught in U.K. classrooms. He is more confident of his place in society.

The monolingual may have no such clues as to the role of language in school life. He comes to school *believing that he speaks the language of the school* so when he fails to access meaning in lessons he sees this as a **failure of his intelligence** rather than a failure of language performance itself.

Research at Bristol university shows that today children from Black African, Chinese, Pakistani, Indian and Bangladeshi backgrounds are outperforming their white counterparts in almost every local authority's figures for 'value added scores'. (Times Educational Supplement 09/02/07). The same study shows that the figures for other categories of black pupils were more mixed.

In addition, what are described as 'poor white working class boys' are reported to have worse GCSE results than their counterparts from any other ethnic background. Senior research officer Dr. Deborah Wilson points out that these results are fairly uniform across the whole country. Again this to me indicates a common basic reason for poor results. Dr. Wilson says that this may be reason may depend on pupil aspiration. I would suggest an additional possibility.

Teacher perception and expectation also play a role.

For a human to really help another human with acquiring language they must first perceive such a need. One can most likely assume that these white children are monolinguals. Of the black pupils other than African black, I assume (without further research to prove or disprove the above two assumptions) that these pupils are mainly English speaking, from a British or Caribbean background.

But far from being an *ethnic* identity issue the figures for me highlight a ***purely language*** issue. The English speaking boy does not see that

Conclusion

the language of school is not the language he speaks at home. He does not know that he has to make *the same effort as a bilingual* to access knowledge in school. His teachers do not understand his language gap, and therefore do not give him the help that they would normally give to someone like a bilingual whom they can see having difficulty. He ends up excluded from understanding much of the work around him.

Exclusion from a group is boycotting. It leads to frustration and boredom. The two year old throws a tantrum when he is alienated by language, and is unable to communicate clearly with his minders. How much more devastating is the anger of a young teenager in much the same isolating position. Alienated by language, slowly but surely innumerable students are excluded from inclusion in school curricula.

So it is not unexpected that in the U.K. fewer children 'like school a lot' (81%) than children elsewhere in the world.

I'm not surprised. I can easily imagine the sheer boredom, frustration and humiliation of sitting through hours, weeks, months of lessons I can never understand. It must build great resentment.

So, with regard to language learning we need to acknowledge the following:-

1. Children require more skilled speakers on whom to model their early attempts at language. They require adults who will make every effort to untangle and interpret their early speech, and having done so to lead them to develop these skills in every way possible.

2. Initially it takes *months* for a new word to become part of a speaker's active – as opposed to passive – vocabulary. Although this acquisition time speeds up considerably with growing intelligence, it takes still takes *years* for children to become aware of, and use, *all* of their linguistic capabilities.

3. Learners need 'scaffolding' to understand subject specific words. Just as adult speech was adjusted to suit the stage of development and comprehension level of the child, so the academic language vocabulary and grammar structures must be selected to match.

4. Children's language skills change every time they meet and cope with a new experience. As human beings, we are all the time learning and relearning language and ways of expressing ourselves. Computers are notoriously difficult to programme to produce language. This is because

they cannot instantly adapt to changing circumstances – whereas humans can.

5. To internalise new vocabulary the child needs to ***actively use it himself***, and not just accept it passively as part of the teacher's or text book's language. A child gets the opportunity to do this when he works collaboratively with his peers. Collaborative work also teaches social skills. It must be very saddening for parents and teachers to see that a 2007 Unicef report reveals that only just 40% of over 11s in the U.K. found their peers to be 'kind and helpful'. This was the worst score in the developed world!

6. Most people, whether conscious of the fact or not, subscribe, in one way or another, to the hidden power agenda of CALP. Those responsible for educating the young, parents, teachers and governmental bodies, create much of their own social problems when they ignore the fundamental role of language in the process.

7. Language is of vital importance to intelligence, its use and development, because most thinking is carried out in verbal form. That is why one of the greatest gifts a parent or teacher can give a child is the help he needs to acquire full fluency.

The End

ISBN 142512277-9